NO EXCUSES

NO EXCUSES

GROWING UP DEAF AND ACHIEVING
MY SUPER BOWL DREAMS

DERRICK COLEMAN JR.
with MARCUS BROTHERTON

GALLERY BOOKS

JETER PUBLISHING

New York   London   Toronto   Sydney   New Delhi

Gallery Books/Jeter Publishing
An Imprint of Simon & Schuster, Inc.
1230 Avenue of the Americas
New York, NY 10020

First Gallery Books hardcover edition June 2015

GALLERY BOOKS and colophon are registered trademarks of
Simon & Schuster, Inc.

For information about special discounts for bulk purchases,
please contact Simon & Schuster Special Sales at
1-866-506-1949 or business@simonandschuster.com.

The Simon & Schuster Speakers Bureau can bring authors to your
live event. For more information or to book an event, contact the
Simon & Schuster Speakers Bureau at 1-866-248-3049 or
visit our website at www.simonspeakers.com.

Interior design by Jaime Putorti

Manufactured in the United States of America

10   9   8   7   6   5   4   3   2   1

Library of Congress Cataloging-in-Publication Data is available.

ISBN 978-1-4767-9658-1
ISBN 978-1-4767-9659-8 (ebook)

For all who need to overcome adversity

CONTENTS

1

FIELD DREAMS

One game.

That's all I ever dreamed of playing.

One game in the NFL—and it couldn't be a preseason game—it had to be one regular season NFL game. For years, my sole focus was making that dream a reality.

I'd be satisfied after playing only one game, too. If they cut me after that, I'd still have peace of mind that I played in the NFL. If all went well and I stayed on the team, then great, I'd set new goals after that. But all I wanted to do was show people I belonged up there—at the highest level. I knew I needed to do everything I could to make that dream come true.

Hey—I didn't even know what I'd even *do* once I got to that game. You might think I had it all figured out—how I'd pictured myself suiting up and running out of the tunnel into a stadium full of screaming fans. How I'd sprint down the field after the kickoff and charge straight for the guy who'd caught the ball and tackle him hard. How I'd play my heart out and be a beast and at least once during that one game get my hands on the football and help my team win.

But I didn't have my dream all figured out. I just wanted to get there and see it unfold. My dream of playing in one NFL game was sort of like a guy driving his dream car—if only for a moment. Maybe it's a Dodge Viper. You don't know exactly what you're going to do with that Viper. But if someone hands you the keys, you'll turn the ignition and screech out of the parking lot with the pedal to the floor.

I was so close to my dream. So close. But one thing stood in my way. This was the third and final day of the NFL Draft. The clock was ticking against me. You can go to the draft in person if you want. It's held at Radio City Music Hall in New York City every year. But most players don't go unless they're a contender for a top pick.

I grabbed four bottles of icy-cold Gatorade out of the kitchen refrigerator at my dad's house in Fullerton, just another middle-class suburb of Los Angeles, and went outside to the driveway, where I was shooting hoops with my friends from the high school days. We were just fooling around playing two-on-two and H-O-R-S-E, and I tossed a bottle each to my friends. We're all fierce competitors and were all drenched in sweat, but I think out of kindness they were letting me win this late in the afternoon. They knew my heart was pounding in my chest and had been since the draft had started two days earlier. They knew I was just waiting for that one big phone call today—either from my agent or from a team—saying, You're it, man. We want you for our team. Welcome aboard. You're in the NFL.

But so far, no phone call.

And time was running out.

My buddies and I all drank our Gatorade and played another quick burst of two-on-two on the driveway, but my mind wasn't in it. Mostly just then, my mind was focused on making a run to the bathroom. That Gatorade had really flown through my system, and my back teeth were floating. All the adrenaline I was feeling at waiting for a phone call wasn't helping any, either.

I went inside the house but the nearest bathroom was occupied, so I passed through the kitchen and the living room to get to the other bathroom. By going through the living room, that meant I needed to look at the TV.

I absolutely did not want to look at the TV.

I was trying so hard to avoid it. The draft is all about anticipation—and I hate anticipation. I can't even watch a television series when it's shown on regular TV if it's one of those shows that have a cliffhanger and are continued every week. I need to know what's happening right now, so I'd far rather download a whole TV series off iTunes and watch it all at once. Too much anticipation, and it feels like my heart's going to explode. That's how I'd feel on game day, too, right before a big game. Anticipation.

Sure enough, I couldn't help but glance at the TV. I couldn't believe we were already at the sixth round. I'd hoped to be picked in the fourth or fifth. Maybe even as high as the third. I figured

I wouldn't go in the first or second, but I'd made the mistake of mentioning my doubts two days earlier to my mama, who's always full of faith. She slapped me upside the head with a serious grin and said, "You never know, Derrick. You might go in the first or second. God is amazing."

And I said, "Yes, he is, but I'm being realistic, too."

I love my mama with all my heart. My dad, too. I'm blessed to have a big network of supporters, family, and friends, but I've gotta say that my mama, May Hamlin, and my dad, Derrick Coleman Sr., are my two biggest supporters. They've worked with me for so many years to get me to the level I'm at. They're my biggest fans, and they've always been pushing me forward, encouraging me, helping me in any way possible. I could never repay them, and I never want to let them down. Particularly not with the draft.

For this third and final day of the draft, I'd wanted to keep the party small at the house. My parents invited my aunts and uncles, my grandparents, and some friends over to the house—that was it. They were all watching the TV except my grandma, who was in the kitchen, frying some chicken for supper. Everyone's mouth was watering at the smell of that fried chicken. The counters were piled high with potato salad and Doritos and chips and baked beans and fresh coleslaw. Plenty of warm apple pie was waiting for dessert. My grandma is the best cook ever. She cooks on point. But there I was, glancing at the TV while on my way to the bathroom, and my heart sank in my chest. The draft was too far along. The clock was ticking too quickly. I should have been picked by now. Something was wrong. Definitely wrong.

We'd all known I stood a high chance of getting drafted.

I wasn't a Heisman winner or anything, and I knew I wouldn't be a first-round pick, but I knew I stacked up well against other college running backs, and I was confident that I'd proved myself both on and off the field.

I was a senior at the University of California, Los Angeles, a standout player on my team. My stats as a running back were really strong. My game film had been sent everywhere. My senior year alone I led the team with eleven touchdowns. I was ranked second on my team with a career-best 765 yards rushing. I'd won the Tommy Prothro Award for Outstanding Special Teams Player, and the Paul I. Wellman Memorial Award for All-Around Excellence. My coaches and agents and friends and family all agreed that I had a strong shot at making the NFL, a really strong shot. But if I wasn't picked by now . . . well . . . this thought rushed at me as terrifyingly as a veteran linebacker, huge, agile, and fast—maybe I wasn't going to get my one game after all. Maybe I was going to let down my friends and family. Maybe my dream was never going to come true. I quickly walked past the TV, went and did my thing, then washed up and headed back outside.

Mama was sitting in the garage with her phone in her hands. The garage door was up, and she was watching us play basketball, but not really. She was praying, waiting, wanting with all her might for that phone to ring, just like we all were. I looked her way and she smiled at me, but her smile was tense. No call had come. Who were we kidding?

I was never going to play in the NFL.

You gotta realize the odds against me making it even this far—
I mean, as far as I'd gotten that Saturday in April—playing basketball on my driveway, waiting for the phone to ring, hoping and
praying like mad that I was going to get drafted into the NFL.

The process of making it to the NFL starts back in high school.
Actually, it starts even before that, in a sense, but high school is
where the road to the NFL becomes more serious. Think about
how many high school football players there are at any given time
in the United States. We all love football in America. It's played on
every high school field and playground patch of grass from coast to
coast and back again, New York to Los Angeles, Miami to Seattle.

If you're playing at a high school level, then football is competitive, but there's still fun and games involved, too. It's a bit more
relaxed. A lot of the guys have played in middle school and for Pop
Warner leagues, so they know what's going on. But a lot of guys
are still learning the fundamentals of the game, even by the time
they reach high school. A couple of players on each high school
team will be really good. One might be a standout player. Most of
the other guys will soon learn to hold their own. But at that level a
few players on your team will be average. A few players might even
suck. So, let's do a little math. There are about 37,000 high schools
in America. Most high schools are going to have football programs.
Each high school team has about 50 players. That's about 1.8 million high school players total. That's where the pool of potential
NFL players begins—a pool as big as the ocean is wide.

The years pass, and you need to narrow that pool to a river.
Plenty of high school seniors want to play football at a college level,
which you have to do to make it into the NFL. With other pro-

fessional sports, like basketball, for instance, a guy can sometimes jump straight from high school to the big leagues. But not football. In football, you either have to play a minimum of three years in college to be eligible—or you have to be out of high school for three years. They want you older, bigger, tougher, wiser. That's how it works. So, you take those 1.8 million high school players, and maybe a quarter of them will be high school seniors. That means some 460,000 high school seniors are trying to make the jump and play at a collegiate level. Colleges want the best players they can get, and here's where the first real sharp ax falls.

You quickly see at college how that's where the business side of the game kicks in. In college, you have to keep your scholarship, and to do that you have to play well. Most players will have mastered the fundamentals of the game by then, but not everything about the game will be mastered. Football's a game where you keep learning as long as you play it. It's sorta like golf. When you watch it on TV, it looks so easy. But then you try to play the game yourself. The slightest repositioning of your arm, your elbow, your legs, your back, can make the difference between a ball in the sand trap and a hole in one. The stakes are raised in college. Definitely raised.

About 115 colleges across America have NCAA Division 1 football programs. Each college team has about 110 players. Division 2 has about the same amount of teams. There's also Division 3 to contend with, as well as NAIA. So, you take that original ocean of high school players, and maybe you end up with 40,000 college players total, with a quarter of those positions becoming open each year to freshmen as the college seniors graduate. That's 1.8 million high school players getting sliced down to about 10,000 college freshmen who get to play football. Point being: It ain't easy to play football at a college level. And after that, it gets even harder.

If you want to play in the NFL, then part of the challenge means you gotta survive three years in college. Football's brutal. I respect a man if he becomes a lawyer or an architect, a doctor or a journalist—all of those are competitive professions where you have be really good to make it. But the big difference between any of those and football is that in those professions no one's trying to physically hurt you like they do when you play the game.

They talk about the "beast" mentality being necessary to play football well. Out there on the field, you gotta be an animal. It's controlled aggression, yeah, but it's most definitely aggression. You can't hold anything back. I know of guys who'll mentally prepare themselves before a game by rehearsing in their minds the time in their lives when they've been the most angry. They get that image in their heads, and then they charge out onto the field, ready to unleash all that rage in the game. That's what's coming toward you every play. It's a street fight. A wall of angry muscle.

If, by chance, you do survive and end up as a college senior and you're not limping or in a coma in a hospital, then you'll find yourself one of about 3,500 other players who potentially could play at the NFL level. Those are the guys you're competing against to make it into the draft. There are also guys from other countries who become eligible for the draft, and they're trying to get spots, too. I'd seen how Tyrone Crawford was drafted by the Cowboys. He's a Canadian. The Giants picked up Markus Kuhn, a star player from Germany. A couple of other standout Canadians were picked up, and a couple of guys from England, too. So the draft is really a worldwide competition, although the bulk of players get drafted from American college teams.

Here's where the numbers really shrink. That river turns into a garden hose. There are 32 NFL teams total. Each NFL team has 53 guys on the roster. That's 1,696 players total in the NFL, give or take, at any one time. Each year, about 200 of those spots open up, so just over 250 guys are ever drafted into the NFL in any given year. Even if you're drafted, that doesn't mean you've made it. The guys who are drafted need to compete with everyone else on the roster as well as the free agents and any guys from other leagues who might be trying for a slot. You could be drafted and still not ever play an official NFL game.

Those are the odds. You start with 1.8 million high school players and time goes by and you cut and cut and finally end up with 250 guys getting drafted. Or think about it this way: There's plenty of good-sized cities in America that have a population of about 68,000 people. If every single person in that city was trying to make it into the NFL, then you'd end up with one draftee out of that city. By the time anybody gets to the NFL level, every player on every team is a great athlete, the best of the best. He's the American idol of the football field. And I was confident I had what it takes to play in the NFL.

But still that phone of mine wasn't ringing.

I went back to the driveway, and my friends and I played some more basketball. We were all practicing our dunks now, all trying to look cool, all trash-talking each other and trying to be the man. In my mind, I thought about how there was one other obstacle I needed to overcome. The thought flashed at me suddenly, because usually I don't even think about it anymore. My friends don't, either. Maybe, I thought, just maybe, that's why my phone wasn't ringing.

See, I never really looked at this other thing as all that big a deal, but I knew other people did if they didn't know me. To me, this other thing was something that always made me stronger. Something that made me so all-fired determined to succeed at the highest level I could. Ever since I was a kid, if ever I wanted to do something, then thanks to this obstacle I'd needed to fight and scrape and claw my way forward, and go as absolutely hard as I could to achieve a goal. When I lifted weights in practice, I lifted like a man on fire. Whenever it was game day and I ran for the ball, I sprinted like a cheetah hungry for a gazelle. If someone was yelling at me, telling me that I was no good, well, I just never listened. You know what I mean?

Let me explain it another way. The day after my Pro Day (where NFL scouts came to UCLA), my agent and his girlfriend were in San Diego doing some business for another client. While there, they were hanging out in a restaurant having beers with two scouts. I won't name the scouts, and to this day, I don't know who they were. But it don't matter none.

My agent says, "What do you think of Coleman?"

And one of the scouts says, "Coleman. Wow, what an impressive Pro Day he had. He's a top physical specimen, all right, he's got the build and moves of an NFL player, but we won't touch him. Sorry to say, but it's the truth."

"How come?" asks my agent. He's got a hunch what they're getting at, but he wants to hear them say it straight out.

"Because we can't take a chance on him, that's how come," says a scout.

The two scouts leave to go to the bathroom or something, and my agent's girlfriend says quietly, just to him, "Can they actually do that? Can they discriminate against a guy like that?" Because she knows what they're talking about.

And my agent says, "Yeah. Of course they can. This is football."

What he means is, if you're in the NFL, then your only job is to win. It doesn't matter if you're a scout, coach, general manager, or player. Your job depends on it. A line like that could bother a guy, sure. It's frustrating to put in all that work and be dismissed, particularly since I'd proved myself in other ways. But I refuse to let something like that bother me. I get what he's pointing at. If you take all the players vying to be in the NFL, and one of them has this one other thing, see, this one strike against him, even if he had nothing to do with that strike being against him in the first place, then they think, Why gamble? Football is just business. It's big business. And everyone involved needs to win.

In fact, my agent has answered that question before—and he's answered it well. Rick Neuheisel, my coach at UCLA, served as a reference point to anyone who asked. We've never tried to hide this one other thing. We shot information about me to all thirty-two NFL teams, saying Rick is able to answer any questions about me and my performance on or off the field. I've never once missed an assignment, that's what Rick told them. I'm able to play the game at the highest level—he told them that, too. Because of this one other thing, I'd work harder, stay out later, come in earlier, lift and push and squat and sprint and throw and catch and run with every ounce of determination I have.

Rick will tell ya.

Never once has it been an impediment to the game that I'm legally deaf.

————

Toward the middle of the sixth round, my phone rang.

We stopped playing basketball immediately. Mom stood up from the chair where she was sitting. I picked up my phone and motioned to everybody to be quiet.

"Hello?" I said.

My heart sank. Instantly, I knew it was nothing. It was just a guy asking me if anybody else had called. He was from a team, sure, but it didn't mean anything.

I hung up, and we went back to playing basketball.

Oh, sure, I'd talked to a lot of teams earlier—Detroit, Oakland, Seattle, and more. A few had flown me out so they could meet with me. A few just talked to me on the phone. They'd said things like "You're definitely on our board. We're definitely interested in you." But I knew that could be a lot of bull, too. You just never know. I felt excited to hear those words from them, but I was trying hard not to set myself up for disappointment, too.

There in the driveway, I reflected back on how a ton of work happens before the draft, and how those three important days are the culmination of all that preliminary work. Just like in any other sport, all the professional football teams have scouting departments, and each year all through the year the team owners put big money into finding talent. Scouts are going out all the time, watching games, looking at film, going to training camps, reading news stories—all the time they're watching players, both on and off the field.

After the regular season, the NFL holds what's called the Scouting Combine, where they bring a bunch of college players to Indianapolis for a six-day assessment. They put the players on the field and give them all these physical and mental tests and interviews just to see how they do. And then each university holds what's called a Pro Day, which is like a combine just for that university's players, and scouts come in to see how you do. On top of that there are all these all-star games where they can look at you, too. So that's all in preparation for the draft.

I hadn't been invited to Combine, which devastated me because I knew how big that was—a high percentage of the guys who go to Combine get drafted. But it isn't unusual for a player not to go to, either. It just made me work harder. I'd done well at UCLA's Pro Day, and I'd played in one of the all-star games and done well there. At my Pro Day, Sherman Smith, the running back coach for the Seattle Seahawks, was there, and he said, "Hey, when you're done, meet me in the auditorium for an interview." So we had a good talk there, about how it's just as important who you are off the field as it is who you are on the field. I don't think we even talked much about football. He asked me all about my family. He wanted to know what kind of person I was. He asked me about my faith. It felt like a good interview all around. After Pro Day I got some more calls from teams.

But a good Pro Day doesn't guarantee you a spot in the draft—that's for sure. What made matters difficult for me was that when I played in the all-star game, they asked me to play fullback to see how that would go for me. I'd always played a different position—running back, more specifically tailback—so there I was in the week before the game, watching all these YouTube videos about how to play fullback.

See, the term *running back* is a broad one. It actually encompasses more than one position. There's the tailback, guys like Marshawn Lynch of the Seahawks and Jamaal Charles of the Chiefs. Those are the big names, the guys who line up seven yards deep and get the handoff. A tailback gets the ball more often. He runs more. He gains yards and even scores more.

Then there's the fullback, which is also a running back position, but it takes different technique, different moves. With a fullback, basically you line up in front of the tailback and block for him. Your job is to create a path for the guy behind you, the guy with the ball. A fullback must be big, strong, and tough. Think of a fullback as a battering ram. It's not a position that a lot of teams even have anymore, since a lot of teams have transitioned to more of a passing game now. Playing fullback is sometimes thought of as a dying art. But a number of teams still value the position, too. See, whenever a team passes the ball, you're taking a lot of chances with that ball flying through the air—interceptions, fumbles, you name it. But when you run the ball, you keep the ball close to the ground, and the play stays more controlled. That's the benefit that a good fullback can bring to a team—he opens the door and strengthens the running game. He helps guarantee yardage. That's why they wanted me to try playing it.

When I was told to play fullback, I didn't like that personally—hey, I'd played running back for eight years already—but I kept my mouth shut. My dad always told me that nobody likes a whiner. There wasn't anything I could do about it, either. What am I going to say to them? No—not interested? Of course I was interested, and I tried to keep my big goal in mind. I just wanted to play football, and I would do whatever it took to play. I knew that in the position of fullback, I wouldn't get to see the ball as much as possible, but I was up for anything. You tell me to play fullback, and I'll play fullback.

So we went through a week of practice to get ready for the all-star game, and I think I did okay in practice. I was always good at special teams in college, so I was doing punt formations and showing other guys what to do, and the coaches and scouts saw that. One or two of them indicated that I'd absolutely make the NFL for my skills in special teams, which, if you're unfamiliar with that term, means the guys who go onto the field for plays involving a kick of the football. So I felt good about that. I was even elected captain for the all-star game, and the game itself went well. I played well.

After the all-star game, I just went home, kept training, and waited for the draft.

Roughly a month before the draft, team officials meet in secret closed-door meetings. Each team's got what they call the "war room," and that's where the scouts come in and make a case for who they like and why.

Maybe you saw that movie *Moneyball*, a few years back, about the Oakland Athletics baseball team, and how their general manager, Billy Beane, and the assistant GM, Peter Brand, a numbers wiz, totally turned tables on the scouting and selection process and looked at statistics only. That approach certainly worked that year for the A's, but that was baseball. In football the process is still more subjective. A lot of it hinges on how they feel in their gut.

In the war room there are the local area scouts, the cross-check scouts, the college directors, and the general manager, and they might have all gone out and looked at a player and analyzed the stats, or they might have called in a player and had him do a private workout. All the time, they're asking themselves if a guy can do the job. They want height, weight, speed. Those are the three big categories that every player's got to have—and I knew I had those three for sure. I'm six feet tall, 233 pounds, and I can run a forty-meter sprint in 4.52, which is an impressive number for somebody as big as me. But after that—that's where the art of the draft comes to the table.

They might look at who a guy is off the field. Has he had any arrests? Does he have an alcohol problem or an addiction to gambling? Is he going to make trouble for a team if he's signed?

They'll definitely be looking at the pool of prospective players with an eye to who they need right now, and even who they'll need next season. Maybe they want to bring a player in as a backup, because they know one of their starters is injury-prone. You just never know.

My off-field life was in order.

All the rest of that subjectivity I couldn't control.

I just needed to wait for a phone call.

Oh sure, there were some other options. If I didn't get drafted, then my agent would help me figure that out. I might go play in Europe for a season. I might play in the CFL. I might need to go stock shelves for $5.50 an hour like Kurt Warner did when he wasn't drafted in 1994.

But being drafted is definitely everyone's first choice. If you get drafted, then it means that a team wants you. They target you for a reason. You fill a need they have and you're less likely to be cut. If you get drafted you also get a signing bonus. In the first couple of rounds, it can be big, millions. Anywhere past third round, and that bonus is still maybe $30,000 to $70,000—which to me was big money coming straight out of college. I most definitely wanted to get drafted. And the money wasn't the biggest reason, either. Plain and simple, it was my dream—that's what I wanted to achieve.

I could smell Grandma's cooking wafting from the kitchen to outside, but my stomach was all tied up in knots. Too much time had passed. I set the ball down and looked at my friends. I checked my phone again just to see if I'd missed something. I looked at Mama. She shook her head.

Grandma follows that timeless saying "Don't count your chickens before they're hatched." I thought about a twist to that. You know what I'd say to any college player who ever assumes he's a shoo-in for the draft?

I'd say, "Don't buy that BMW."

That was going to become my advice from here on out. It means there are some really talented players out there who don't make the draft. There ain't no guarantee, even if you have good stats, strong game film, and Coach Rick backing you up.

One time I was sitting in this little hole-in-the-wall restaurant near the gym where I work out, and this guy who works for a BMW dealership walks in. We've talked before, and he sits down and tells me about this other football player, a pretty good friend of mine who I played against a couple times in college, and how he tried to buy a car from their dealership,

This other guy is a real beast and his stats are great, and he was absolutely certain he was going to be drafted within the first three rounds. Everyone was telling him this, and he's reading about it in the blogs and stuff, and the news has gone to his head. So he walks into a BMW dealership before the draft, picks out a brand-new Series 7 BMW, and says to the salesman, "I'll take it." The sticker price on the window is $141,000 plus tax. He's that confident. I mean, the guy doesn't even dress up to go to the dealership. He's just wearing old sweats and a T-shirt. I don't know about you, but if ever I go buy a BMW, I'll be certain to dress the part. That's how the world works.

Well, they just laughed at him. Turned him down cold. The guy gets mad and says to the salesman, "I'm about to go first-round draft. I'll show you." He whips out his cell phone and calls his agent. Seems he's got some money stashed in an account somewhere, so he leaves the dealership, goes to the bank and takes out all his money in cash, comes back to the dealership, and says, "That's my car. Gimme the keys." He ain't worried, because he's so sure. He buys the car. But guess what—

He didn't get drafted.

Later, he signed as a free agent, so it worked out for him in the end. But it took a while, and he took the long road to get there. That's why I'd say, "Don't buy the BMW." Don't ever do anything until after your name is called. And—look at the odds—your name probably isn't going to get called.

Mine wasn't getting called.

The sun over Los Angeles was starting to head for the horizon, and my phone was dead in my hands, as dead as my dream. When it came to the 2012 NFL Draft, I was most certainly not going to be picked. My dream was over.

I knew it now beyond the shadow of a doubt.

2

MY START IN LIFE

If you want to play professional football at the highest level, then you've gotta develop a mindset where you hold to both competitiveness and compassion. It's a strange combination, and you have to have a lot of both—and I'm not talking about having this mindset toward the teams you're playing against. I'm talking about having competitiveness and compassion for your own teammates.

When it comes to compassion, you need to care about what happens to another player. You all want to come together as a team, yeah, both on the field and off. And you need to respect a teammate to do that. You all want to play your hearts out as one, and when you do so, you aren't seeking your own glory. You want your team to win. You want to be champions all together. Plus, you want to be able to hang out with your teammates after hours, just kicking back, relaxing or whatever. You want to respect the guy whose locker is next to yours.

But that same player, the guy on your team who you respect and even look up to, may well be the guy you're trying to beat out of a job. He's playing against you sometimes, too. He wants to outshine you. And you want to do the same to him.

That's because teams don't bring in just one guy for a position and hand him the job. They'll bring in two or three or even four guys and have them all scrap for it. It's nothing personal. It's just business.

If you want to be a starter, then you not only need to make the team; once you're on the team, you need to win the position, too. And if you're a starter, the team owners and the managers and the coaches never want you to grow comfortable with your position, not in the sense that you ever get to thinking your job is a sure thing. When it comes to football, you can never phone in your performance. You always need to be playing your hardest.

Keeping your job depends on it.

———

Looking back now, I think I learned part of that dynamic when I was just a kid—at least I sensed that dynamic of strength and uneasiness within my heritage. When it came to security both on and off the field, I needed to fight to claim security, just like those who had gone before me, just like my parents and grandparents did. I needed to develop nerves of steel and a faith in the rock that doesn't move. And that would come by one means only.

By going through challenges.

I don't care who you are or what goal you're trying to achieve, if you've never gone through hard times, then your character's never been tested. Only by going through hard times will you know the stuff you're truly made of.

That's the way it was for my father and my mother. Each of them could write an entire book themselves on the experiences they had while growing up. Both of them went through seasons of hardship, that's for sure. They haven't always made the right choices, but they've learned from their mistakes, and they've come out stronger and wiser for it in the end. I respect that a lot. Even while fighting for their own places in the world they developed an ability to care deeply—that combination of competitiveness with compassion.

I'm closer to my father's parents, Gwen and John Coleman, than to my other set of grandparents, who are passed away now. I never met them and didn't know them at all. Grandma and Grandpa Coleman met and married in Louisiana in 1960 and had three sons: Chico, Darnel, and my dad, Derrick Coleman Sr.

Times were tough for black families in the Deep South in 1960. It was the height of the civil rights era, and lots of families were struggling, lots of folks were dirt poor. But Grandpa and Grandma Coleman were one of the few fortunate families in that regard.

Grandpa Coleman was one of nine children, and they never had much growing up, but as an adult he worked his way up by grit and determination to become the chief assistant engineer for a company called IPT Continental, which basically meant he worked in a bakery making Wonder Bread.

Grandma Coleman worked for the federal government. She

was raised in a small town not far from him and they met in high school. Her mom, my great-grandmother, was a schoolteacher, and both her mom and dad had passed away when she was a little girl, so my grandmother was raised by her grandmother. After my grandma and grandpa Coleman had my uncle Chico, they moved from Louisiana to Los Angeles, where Grandpa drove a cab. They bought a middle-class suburban home in South Bay, on the outskirts of Carson and Gardena. Grandma still lives there today.

They had a close family as their kids were growing up—and it's still close today. The adversity they felt in the outside world made them feel somehow that much more sheltered at home. Grandma made her kitchen a refuge for herself and others. For years on end, they'd invite over a bunch of family and friends every holiday, and she'd do the cooking. To this day we still have maybe a hundred folks over at her house every Christmas and Thanksgiving. Grandma cooks up a real southern feast—ham, turkey, stuffing, greens, peas, potato salad, ambrosia, yams (that's my favorite, along with Grandma's mac and cheese), gravy, cranberry sauce, and for dessert, all kinds of cakes and pies. It's a real party. That's something you should know about us: the Coleman family loves to cook. Which also means the Coleman family loves to *eat*!

Grandpa Coleman was a humble, quiet man, and my dad, Derrick Sr., is a lot like him nowadays. I like to think some of those traits have been passed on to me, too. I've never heard my grandfather or father yell or curse, and that's saying a lot about a man these days. Sure, everyone gets upset, including my grandfather and father, and they might whisper a strong word under their breath if they hit their thumb with a hammer or something, but I've never heard them use profanity in regular conversation, and I've never, ever heard them use strong language when they're around women or kids.

My father describes himself as an adventuresome kid while growing up, and fairly quiet, which he still is, although he's in the Toastmasters today, so he does a lot of public speaking. When he was a kid, he was always busy doing something, usually outside, playing baseball, football, tennis, basketball, running races—usually just out on the street, usually just my dad and his two older brothers playing together. Grandpa Coleman saw the value of strength conditioning, so he made a weight bench for his three boys, and they used to work out in their backyard. My dad works out regularly today and is still really strong. He and I worked out together for years, and I have him to thank for a lot of the strength I have developed today.

My mother's family is nowhere as close as my dad's side of the family.

My grandmother on my mother's side had eight kids by my maternal grandfather, but my mother's folks were never married any of that time. I guess my maternal grandmother's family didn't like my grandfather much, so they were estranged as a family toward the man.

It sounds like the family had solid reasons for this distance, although I don't know firsthand because I never met the man. My maternal grandpa was said to be a harsh man who took out his wrath on his own family. Reportedly, he even beat my grand-mother, and I can't stand the thought of a man ever doing that to a woman. She ended up with broken arms, legs, you name it—he did it to her. That's reprehensible. There was also abuse going on against the children, Mom says, and they all pretty much grew up in a single-parent family, with Grandma doing most of the parent-ing. This was in Dallas, where they all stayed then. As tough as that is to hear, that's how it happened.

Mom was the youngest of those eight children, and the one bright spot in Mom's growing-up years was that when she was about nine years old, a friend who lived around the corner took her to church. I guess the friend's family was heavy into church, and it was a Holiness church, so there was always a lot of praising and shouting going on. Grandma took the kids to church, too, when she was able, so Mom grew up with a lot of faith influencing her. Mom describes how she knew that God had His hand on her in good ways, even when she had nothing. God was always leading and guiding my mother, because even when she was going through the real hard times that she did, she could have gone many different ways or turned to so many harmful things, like drugs or alcohol, but she never did. God allowed Mom to stray only so far before He brought her back.

When my mother was twelve, the real hard times began for her. One evening her mother was walking over to a friend's house, and there was an overpass where cars exit the freeway. Grandma was crossing the street when a car hit her. The car dragged her about a hundred feet, and then kept going. Killed her. The police never found out who the driver was.

Mom's dad was still around, but he wasn't fit to raise a twelve-year-old girl by himself, so Mom went to live with an aunt on the other side of Dallas. Mom had all those older siblings she might have gone to live with, but they were all still pretty young themselves, all just trying to live their own lives. Because of the past physical abuse in the family, they were all trying to get out of the house themselves, too, trying to make their own way in the world. So there's distance between those siblings today, partly because they didn't or couldn't step up to the plate for her when she was so young. Mom has met up again with some of them in later years, but I've got a whole bunch of aunts and uncles I've never met, really a whole side of the family I don't know.

Times proved hard at the aunt's house, and Mom had her first baby, my brother, Keyon, when she was only sixteen years old.

Mom kept on living with her aunt, but I guess the relationship was real strained between them because when Mom graduated from high school in 1986, her aunt put her out of the house that same evening. Mom was just seventeen when she graduated. On the night she went to her senior prom, and when she came home, all her stuff was packed for her. That was that. She had nowhere to live, nowhere to go. So Mom moved in with another aunt and then went house to house, working odd jobs, until she finally drifted out to California. When Keyon was two years old, my mom gave birth to my sister, Tenisha, who was fathered by a different man. All this time my mom was trying to figure out how to be a single parent. Sometimes she was homeless, sleeping in her car.

How she did all that by herself is a wonder to me. How she survived. My mama's brave, I'll say that much. Picture a young woman with such a loss of security in her life. Nobody's looking out for her. Nobody's there to give her advice or help her along. Nobody's cherishing her. That's who she was then. That's my heritage.

And then there's how I came to be.

In the summer of 1989, my mom was out at an L.A. club called the Name of the Game, where she happened to meet a young man named Derrick Coleman. (He didn't have the pleasure of being Derrick Coleman, *Senior* . . . yet!) It was casual at the start. Their paths crossed and they started talking. Pretty soon he asked her to dance. They exchanged numbers and went out a couple of more times. Months passed, and at some point they became exclusive, and after that my mother discovered she was pregnant with me. No, they were never married. I know it crossed their minds, and at one point they planned to get married. But at that young age, with me coming into the picture, there didn't seem to be time or money.

My father is a bit older than my mom. He was twenty-three when I was born, right around the same age as I am today, which is pretty young for a man to be raising a family. To hear him describe it, he was just starting to date women seriously and still had a lot to learn about how things work within a loving and committed relationship. Fortunately he'd just started working his way up in a steady job, building aircraft for McDonnell Douglas. At first he was a bit unsure about the pregnancy, but then he warmed up to the idea, and when I was born, he thought I was a real good thing.

Until my dad and mom worked all that out, they were on-again, off-again in their relationship. At one point, just before I was born, Mom said she'd had enough. She loaded up her car with her two toddlers and everything she owned, left California, and moved back to Texas. She drove all night in a rickety old car that she wasn't sure was going to make it. My dad talked her into moving back to L.A. again. They were on friendly terms when she got back, but not living together then. So my mom lived with an aunt for a while, then with a cousin up north, and then in Inglewood with another aunt until it was time for me to be born.

On the morning of October 18, 1990, right before I was born, my mama called my dad and he rushed to the hospital to be there for her, but he ended up getting there just after I'd arrived. Still, he describes the whole experience as a proud moment, a real joyful time. He felt relief, actually, now that I was here. Before I'd arrived, he'd felt fear because the experience of being a father was unknown to him. After I'd arrived, Dad was real proud of me. He says that right away he could see a family resemblance. Pretty soon, whenever he'd hold me and say something, I'd smile.

My mama was happy to see me, too. She suggested that they name me after my dad because she wanted to give me some solidity, some foundation, something she never had. She was still doing a lot of struggling, still trying to figure out how life worked. After I was born, she moved in with my grandmother, my father's mother. They were always best of friends, even when the relationship between my parents was struggling. My dad wanted Mama there, too, because she knew we'd all be safe and well taken care of. So Mom stayed there a week or so, then went back to Inglewood, where we lived for a while.

I was a healthy baby, six pounds, eight ounces—not exactly big, but just a normal, healthy size. Mama doesn't remember how many inches long I was. What she does remember quite clearly is that every time a child is born, the state mandates that the baby have a hearing test. I had that right in the hospital in the nursery, and I passed my hearing test just fine.

I know it might sound a little strange today to hear that I passed that test, but that's what they said, so what else could Mama do about it back then? I don't know if they do it like this anymore, but back then a nurse came and got me, just like they got every newborn baby, and carried me to another room to do the test, so my mama wasn't even present to watch it happen. When they discharged Mama and me from the hospital, all they said was I passed and could hear fine. Why would Mama wonder if anything was wrong?

The only thing that came up even remotely abnormal was during the phenylketonuria test, which they call the PKU—that's where they stick a needle in the baby's heel and draw blood from it. They found out that I had PKU, which meant it was harder for me to break down amino acids in foods that contain protein. I needed to be really careful taking aspirins, too. So that was that. Otherwise, all was well.

After Mama brought me home, things took a turn. I threw up lots more than her other babies ever did. She'd worked in nursing homes and was on track to become a nurse herself, so she had a little medical knowledge already. She took me to the doctor's office, and they said nothing was wrong, but then one day at home I threw up with so much force that my vomit hit the wall. Mom rushed me to the emergency room. The doctor on call asked if I'd lost any weight, which I had, so they admitted me and did a full workup.

It turned out to be pyloric stenosis, a dangerous condition where food gets blocked and can't move from the stomach to the intestine. The very next day after the diagnosis I had surgery. I was only about three weeks old. Mom still talks about the surgeon who worked on me. He was a tall man with huge hands, and Mom says that when she saw him pick me up, I looked so tiny and fragile in those huge hands of his. All of my dad's side of the family came to the hospital and sat with my mom in the waiting room.

After my surgery, which seemed to go okay, I ate everything in sight. But every time after that, if I even so much as spit up, Mama would rush me straight back to the hospital. She was always so afraid. She wasn't that hypervigilant with her other two kids. She was a good mother to them, too, but she was never as worried with them as she was with me.

As a family, we had some definite things to be worried about. When we were staying over at Inglewood and I was in the hospital for my surgery, the house caught on fire. My brother was inside the house, and someone ran inside and rescued him, so he was okay. They got the fire out, but it did a lot of damage to the structure. After the fire, Mama got her own apartment in Gardena. She wasn't working then. She was on welfare. When I got old enough for day care, she went back to school to become a licensed vocational nurse.

It's hard to fully describe the relationship between my parents back then. They loved each other, I've never doubted that, but they just couldn't seem to make it happen. I've never faulted them for that. Mama has always had a close relationship with my dad's side of the family, and she and my grandma Coleman get along well, with lots of love, just like she's her real daughter. Even though my parents have been so on-again, off-again through the years, they decided early on they would always pull together when it came to me.

I like that. I like that a lot. We were a strange sort of family in a lot of ways. Separated parents. A couple of kids from other relationships. Two addresses. Parents trying to make it at work. A family trying hard to struggle up that ladder to make a better way in life. But maybe we're like a lot of families today, when you think of it. We never had much, but we weren't starving. We didn't look like a conventional family, but we always had a lot of love. Grandma Coleman used to say, "When you got love, then you're rich. When you got your family that cares about you, then that's what you really need."

So that was my start in life. Some strikes against me from the start, sure, some challenges I needed to overcome right from day one.

Yet I was also blessed with a lot of love, a lot of hope, and a lot of dreams about something far better to come.

3

HOW IT ALL BEGAN
TO GO WRONG

I was a hyperactive baby. Mom tells me I got into a lot of things as a toddler. One day when Mom wasn't looking I pulled the clothes iron down on me and burnt my leg. Mom rushed me to the hospital, but she was afraid to tell the doctors what had happened because she hadn't been in the room with me when the accident happened. My older brother saw it happen, so he was able to tell the doctors that Mama wasn't abusing me or anything like that.

Far from it. Mama loved me with a fierceness, and I loved Mama right back. Mostly I was a cheerful, happy kid who loved to smile. I was definitely active. Always on the move. For a while Mama thought I had ADHD because I was all over the place.

When I was not even two years old, I went over to Grandma Coleman's house for an Easter egg hunt. I had on my Sunday blue shorts and a white shirt. The backyard was swarming with kids, and I didn't quite understand what we were all supposed to do. But I got in my head that we were supposed to run around and pick things up, and that we were competing against other kids to see who could pick up the most eggs. Fine with me. I ran as hard as I could, just barreling into kids and knocking them over, many of them far bigger than me.

When the hunt was finished, somebody glanced at Mama and said—and this quote is verbatim, maybe even prophetic—"When that kid grows up, he's going to be a football player."

I loved playing with toy trucks and airplanes. Whatever I could put my hands on, I would throw it or bang it. But I wasn't fearless. For my second birthday, we all went to a Chuck E. Cheese's for games, food, and a big party. If you've never been to a Chuck E. Cheese's, let me explain: it's a really high-octane restaurant for kids, with a lot of bright lights and loud noises and a huge mouse mascot who walks around giving kids high-fives. At Chuck E. Cheese's, I was scared out of my wits. When I first saw that big mouse, I ran across the room and jumped straight into my cousin's lap. Everyone thought it was hilarious. Hey, I was just demonstrating my sprinting ability.

It wasn't all fun and games.

Whenever Mama called my name, I seemed to have a hard time responding to her. Constantly, she needed to say the same thing over and over again. She figured that I was just being hardheaded and a busybody and doing what I wanted to do, ignoring her.

Funny, but it hadn't been that way with her first two kids. They were normal kids all right, and sometimes they did what they were told and sometimes they didn't. But with me, something seemed a bit different, just slightly off. Whenever Mama talked to me, I seemed to respond best if she was using a loud voice. I wasn't bad. I just seemed stubborn. Like if I was playing with my toys and Mama told me to clean up, I did it—and I did it cheerfully—but it would take her telling me to do so seven or eight times before I got it into gear and moved.

Other people noticed the same thing about me, although they responded in different ways. While Mama was studying to be a nurse, I stayed with a babysitter for a time. I don't remember anything about staying with her at all, but one day Tenisha got sick and needed to stay home from school, so that day she went to the same babysitter as me. When Tenisha and I got home, Tenisha told Mama that the babysitter was yelling and screaming at me, cursing me out, because I "wouldn't listen."

Mama was mad at that babysitter. That was the last time I ever went there. But she was worried about me, too. Something was wrong with her little guy, and she didn't know what. I had a little cousin, Danielle, several months younger than me, and Danielle was already speaking but I wasn't. Mama thought maybe it was just because I was a boy and Danielle was a girl, and girls talk more quickly than boys, but she wasn't sure. I had a few words down okay. I could say "no" just fine. I said "Mama," "Daddy," and "Kee-on" for my brother. For my sister, Tenisha, I called her "Tee-on," which was close enough for now.

For some reason, I didn't like it when people touched me—particularly my face and head, anywhere near my ears. My father said I could sometimes be "fussy" like that, almost like I didn't want to be bothered. Maybe it had something to do with my hearing impairment; I'm not sure. I think I was afraid of people in general. No big reason, that's just the way I was. Sometimes I'd even try to bite people if they touched me. Hey—it was the only way I knew how to fight back. One afternoon I was sitting on the counter and Tenisha was playing with me, but I didn't know she was just playing. She came too close to me, so I bit her with my two front teeth right on the nose. It drew blood on poor Tenisha. Fortunately she didn't need any stitches, but she still has a faint line across her nose from that.

I'm not afraid of people anymore. Looking back, I think I spent a lot of years running away from interactions with others. But now my job is the opposite of that. It's to be immersed in a world of people. Actually, my specific job is to run straight toward people—and hit them. How's that for a turnaround? I don't know if there's any big connection there, but I'd say—and this is in all seriousness—that you've got to have versatility in your life. If I didn't like it when people touched me, then I needed to get over that. Everybody's got to be able to change, adapt, do whatever's required to carry on in life. Maybe you're really good at cooking on a stove, and somebody asks you to grill on a barbecue. You don't know how to barbecue, so it makes you flustered or nervous or afraid or angry. Then figure out how to use that barbecue, man. Do whatever it takes to get the job done.

Grandma Coleman was working full-time back then, so she wasn't able to look after me much. But sometimes she looked after me on Saturdays, particularly if my dad needed to work overtime. One day after caring for me, Grandma Coleman asked my mama if I'd gotten my hearing tested at the hospital when I was a baby, and of course I had. But maybe I needed to get it checked out again, Grandma said.

Daddy was having similar thoughts. Mama and my daddy shared custody of me, and I got used to being shuttled back and forth from place to place. Daddy always took me to get my haircuts down at a place he liked. The barber's name was Percy, and he was a friend of my father. I always got a fade, we called it, high and tight, trim on the sides and a little on the top.

One Saturday afternoon when I was sitting in the barber's chair, Percy the barber was saying something to me but I wasn't answering him back. I was nearly three years old then, old enough that I should have answered. At first Daddy didn't think much of it, because I wasn't doing much talking yet anyway. But then Daddy noticed that whenever Percy was standing in front of me and asked me a question, I answered quickly. But if Percy was standing in back of me, I didn't answer at all.

When the weekend was over, Daddy compared notes with Mama when they made the swap, and she said she'd take me to get my hearing tested again, although she didn't know where to do that.

Mama says she was nervous about how to proceed. This was all new ground to her, as it would be for any parent. Who do you call? What do you do? Where do you go? It's like a thousand-piece puzzle is set down before you and you need to figure it all out as quick as you can because the health of your child is at stake. I can only imagine how scary that is, thinking that something's probably wrong with your child. You're afraid of what they might find. You're afraid of what might be there but they *don't* find.

Mama ended up taking me over to a local public school. I didn't go to that school, because I wasn't old enough yet, and Mama had health insurance, so she could have taken me to a doctor. But she wanted something done right away, and the school offered free hearing tests. They could see me the next day.

I guess the hearing tests done at the school weren't all that sophisticated. They put me in a booth. It was outside in a trailer, I remember, and they said, "Yeah, something's wrong with him all right." But they couldn't tell Mama the extent of what was wrong with me or why something was wrong. They told us to go to a regular doctor, so Mama made the appointment.

They did another test at the regular doctor's. This test was more extensive, and they said that sure enough, I had some hearing loss in my left ear. They didn't know how much, and they didn't know what was causing it, but they knew for sure that my ear wasn't responding as it should. My right ear had more hearing ability than my left, they said, but it looked to be deteriorating, although they didn't know why, and they didn't know how quickly I was losing my hearing in that ear. I hardly remember anything about that appointment, but to hear Mama tell the story, the response at the doctor's office was basically, "Yeah, here's another kid who's going to be deaf. Deal with it."

Mama didn't know what to do next. She describes how she felt kind of numb for a period of time. Nobody in the family had ever experienced something like this. She didn't have any friends who were hard of hearing. Everything she was facing was new and unknown. She wondered if the hearing loss was from an infection. She wondered if maybe it was progressive, from some kind of disease, and that maybe things were going to get worse for me. But she was having a hard time articulating things at the doctor's. All they told her that I needed to have hearing aids, and that if I was ever going to learn how to speak, then Mama just needed to talk to me all the time. Hopefully my speech was going to develop all right, but they couldn't say if it would for sure.

If you asked Mama today about what she'd do now if ever placed in a similar situation, she'd tell you she would have done as much research as she could even before she went to the doctor's, so she would have known what questions to ask. She'd tell anyone to be as proactive as you can, assertive but not aggressive, and do all you can do to understand. She'd tell you to insist to the doctors that they find the reason behind the disability. She'd ask if there were more tests they could do. She'd push hard for them to figure out if genetics factored into the disability, or if something went wrong during birth. My mama's a nurse herself now, and she loves her job. Yet she'd tell you that sometimes people who are in positions of authority, including those in the medical profession, might brush off a young parent and dismiss them as afraid, or uniformed, or too young, or too worried. But she'd also say that, as a new parent, it's perfectly okay for you to *refuse* to be brushed off like that. Politely press for the answers you need. Tell your doctor you want to go see a specialist. Become educated. Become well-read. This is your child—so become passionate and do whatever's needed for your child, and it will get done. That's what Mama tells people now.

She'd do all that because every parent wants answers. A parent is with that child all the time, and a parent needs to become the main advocate for a child. A parent wants closure on a diagnosis, and a parent wants to know as firmly as possible what to do—and what not to do—in order to go forward.

Make sure you're informed—that's what Mama would tell anybody. Make sure you're not afraid. But back then, Mama was uninformed and afraid—she didn't know any of this and just took whatever the doctors said as if it were gold.

What helped were two things, Mama says. The first was prayer. A lot of prayer. Mama asked God to build within her a strong sense of self—praying every day that she would become a great advocate for her child. She knew she needed to do certain things for her son, so she prayed that God would give her a strong and fearless personality. She prayed that God would instill in her whatever skills and character she needed to meet the challenges of raising me.

The second was resolve. Mama determined to go forward. She knew there were still a lot of unanswered questions about what my life was going to be like. A lot of worries. A lot of fears. But she knew one thing for certain.

She would give it her all.

And she would press on.

We got my first hearing aids from a hearing aid dispensary over in Lakewood. They needed to make molds first, so they could make the hearing aids be a custom fit. It wasn't easy to get me to sit still so they could make the molds, but finally I did.

It took a while for the hearing aids to get made, and then we went back to the dispensary again. My hearing aids were huge, big and brown. You couldn't hide them if you wanted to. It isn't easy to get a three-year-old to stick something in his ears that he doesn't want stuck there, but after a while Mama coaxed those hearing aids in.

When she first put them in, both my mama and daddy say there was a light that went on in my eyes. I smiled really big. Something new was happening inside my head for the first time, and I liked it. I just didn't know what it was. I liked it, but it felt strange, too, so when those contraptions first went in, I smiled but then quickly tried to pull them out. Patiently, Mama walked me through the process again. It took a few days, but after a while I got used to them.

I went to preschool with my hearing aids in. Nobody laughed at me then, that I remember. My favorite clothes were a pair of fire-engine red shorts and a bright green shirt. I must have been quite a sight—this little kid dressed up in Christmas tree colors with these huge brown hearing aids sticking out of his head like bug antennas. I only needed the hearing aid for my left ear at first, but the audiologist told us that I should get used to wearing them both, so that's what we did.

Mama and Daddy both talk about how it was no small task to get an active little boy to wear his hearing aids all the time. They cleaned them for me, put them in and out, changed batteries, everything. It took some work, that's for sure.

Overall, my diagnosis didn't seem to faze my parents much. As a couple, they just knew something was wrong with me, so they resolved to put themselves aside and do whatever it took to get me what I needed. My father's insurance paid for my hearing aids.

Mama and Daddy both describe now how my diagnosis actually helped bring them closer, even though they never married. There was a sense that they needed to work together to make sure I got what I needed. If Mama took me to the doctor, then she always made sure my Daddy knew about it and what was happening. The diagnosis actually opened up their lines of communication. Today, I don't think my mama talks much if at all to the fathers of my other siblings, but she talks to my father all the time. Working to ensure my well-being became a bond between them.

After I got my hearing aids, nobody who looked after me treated me any different. I've asked them about that today, and the answer is a resolute "No." Grandma sure didn't. My mama and daddy didn't. There was no favoritism in our family. You just did what you needed to do. If a kid behaved badly, then he got what was coming to him. When it came to disciplining me, or making sure I minded my manners, or making sure I respected whoever needed respecting, nobody let up on me, that was for sure.

From there on, Mama was always working with me on my speech. For the longest time, nobody could understand me. Whenever I spoke, it was sort of this thick drone. But Mama kept talking to me every chance she got, trying to get me to enunciate my words correctly. I think that's part of the reason I'm so close to my mama today. We were always talking, right from the start.

Learning to talk clearly is no easy task for a hearing-impaired person. Even today, after years of speech therapy, I still sometimes catch myself saying things that don't sound right. Particularly if I get excited or intense over something, I'll say things and realize the words are coming out as mumbling sounds. The correct words are going through my mind, but even I can't understand what I'm saying.

Part of the problem with me moving forward was that as a family we kept moving around a whole bunch. It was hard to get any consistency in audiologists or outside help. If you're not from Los Angeles, you need to understand that basically it's made up of a bunch of smaller cities within the greater metro area. Mama moved from Gardena back to Inglewood again, although this time we were in our own apartment. Inglewood isn't known for being a terribly safe neighborhood. There's gang activity, and Mama never felt safe letting us kids play outside. Then we moved to Lawndale, then to another place in Lawndale, then to Torrance. Those places were all part of Los Angeles, but all different cities within the bigger city.

Mama was working a lot then. Often she worked the night shift. Sometimes we had babysitters. Sometimes it was just my older brother looking after us, to save money. Once, we were getting ready to move again, and Mama told us kids about it, although she didn't tell us when. That night, when she came home after her shift, I'd moved every piece of furniture in my room out into the living room by myself. My bed. My dresser. A chair. I don't know what else I had back then, but it was a bunch of stuff.

Mama just looked at me real quizzically, like, *What you doing?*

And I was like, "I thought you said we were moving."

"Yeah. But not today," she said, and made me put everything back again.

It seemed like whatever happened to me happened in a powerful way. I came down with the chicken pox right around then, when I was about five. It was really bad. There were spots all over my face and around my ears. I'd scratch the spots, and they got infected. My head was so swollen I could hardly wear my hearing aids anymore. Pus and whatever else was draining, just leaking out of me from everywhere, and I was stinking, smelling something awful, so they took me to the hospital. The doctor who examined me said he'd never seen a case of chicken pox as severe as I had. They put an IV in me and put me on antibiotics. Gradually I healed up, though it felt like it took forever.

But life wasn't all bad. I was a muscular little kid. If ever I took my shirt off, you could see I had defined muscles, even from an early age. Early on I was skinny, but pretty soon I started bulking up. My dad and I played all sorts of games in the park around then. He played tennis with me, I remember that well. And he played some basketball with me so I could develop hand-eye coordination. I didn't have the greatest sense of balance and seemed to trip and fall more than most kids. My parents learned later that that's typical when your ears are messed up, because your equilibrium is not what it should be. So Dad helped with that.

I loved going to the park. If ever I could be outside, that's where

I liked being the best. There's a big park in Long Beach, El Dorado Regional Park, and my dad would take me and Keyon down there with our bikes where we rode around in laps. This one loop we rode on was five miles, and I did that no problem, even as a little kid. We might stop and play on the swings for a while. That was always fun.

There were fun times with Mama, too. She was learning more about how to advocate for me, figuring out what was best and how she could urge me forward. One time I was complaining that my chest hurt. A little kid shouldn't be complaining of chest pains, so she took me to the ER. The doctor on call dragged his feet and said nothing was wrong with me. Mama was learning how not to be afraid of doctors, and she told him—in no uncertain terms—to get out of the way. She was going to find another doctor.

And she did. Another doctor came in and saw that my heart rate was low. He sent me to a cardiologist, and eventually it was determined that nothing serious was wrong with me. But the point was that Mama was learning how to be my biggest advocate. If somebody wasn't going to help her when it came to me, then she was going to push forward and go to the next person.

My parents were both committed to taking me with them everywhere. If Mama was home and needed to run errands, she took me with her. My older brother and sister might stay at home, but I would always go. Mama wanted me to interact with as many people as I could. She wanted me to talk to the checkout clerk at the grocery store. She wanted to boost my speaking ability by hearing as many voices as possible. She wanted me to never think of myself as different. That set a good foundation for me. I was going to need it.

Ask her today and she'll tell you that she never wanted me to think of myself as different, because if I did then others would pick up on this—and often, particularly when kids are in school, "different" has a negative connotation. She never wanted me to feel sorry for myself, or like I wasn't good enough. In Mama's eyes, I was God's child—and that was all that mattered.

Mama was feeling this tension herself and she could be fierce for me, although I didn't really realize this until I was older. Hearing-impaired people tend to have a different sound to their voices. My voice tends to be lower, because mostly I only hear bass. So Mama describes how she was constantly on guard that someone would make fun of me or how I talked. The constant vigilance put her on the defense all the time, and she had to watch herself to make sure she didn't overreact because she didn't want to live her life that way, or influence me to do the same.

I don't remember this story personally, but Mama tells how one day we were at the mall and I was acting hyper, jumping around or whatever, so she tried to grab my hand. Right then this guy and his girlfriend walked by, and the guy made some sort of comment like, "See, that's why I don't want to have children." And Mama was like, "Oh no you just didn't." She followed him for a while as they kept walking, saying her piece to him until she made good and sure the guy understood that he'd better not ever say anything bad about her kid!

I went to preschool in Paramount, and we were all living at my dad's house for a while then. I personally don't remember anyone making fun of me in preschool. One of my cousins (he wasn't really my cousin, but our parents worked together, so that's what I called him) was in the same school as me. His name was Andrew, and he was a friend, a true friend. We used to ride our bikes around and race each other, seeing who could reach the end of the sidewalk first.

If you're in preschool, what do you know about girls? I dunno, but I guess Andrew knew something, because he was about four years old and there was this girl he liked, the same age. One day he asked her to go around the side of the preschool because he wanted to kiss her. Maybe it was just to talk with her, I don't know, but the way he built it up to me, whatever they were going to do was going to be really big.

Andrew asked me to keep lookout for him, so I did. The girl seemed to think going around the side of the school was pretty fun, and so did my friend, because when they came back, they were both grinning. That felt good to me. I didn't know a whole lot about friendships when I was that young, but I think it was just one of the first sparks I ever felt that indicated how good and necessary a friendship can be. I felt like in my own small way, I had helped a friend out somehow. No matter how trivial it was. There was a connection made, at least.

The next year in kindergarten was mostly fun, too. I had friends then. I don't remember anything bad about kindergarten, except that it was a different school and Andrew wasn't around. When you're that young, nobody really senses much different in the kid next to him. If somebody's got these things in his ears, well, you don't care. You're five years old. You just want to have fun. And if something has nothing to do with you, then you disregard it. I don't remember anyone making fun of me that year.

Despite my mother's hard life, she's always been full of faith. She describes how prayer was always a big part of the process with me all along. For years Mama prayed that I would be healed and that God would open my ears.

When I was young, a faith healer came to Los Angeles for a three-day event, along with a minister and his wife. I can't vouch for their validity or what goes on within their ministries, but Mama went the first day with some friends from church, and then the second day was a Saturday, so she took me along.

We went over to the big auditorium in the convention center in Anaheim where they were all speaking. We were seated next to the wall, and there was a crowd near the front. The speaker said, If anyone wants to be healed, come forward for prayer. Mama stood up, grabbed my hand, and led me through the crowd straight to the front.

The minister's wife was praying for people, and she came over to where we were and laid hands on me and prayed for me. Mama and I had our eyes closed and our hands up, receiving the blessing. I don't remember that anything miraculous happened right away—but this is true, too: sometimes miracles don't unfold exactly the way you'd think they would.

Like I say, Mama was hoping and expecting that my ears would instantly be opened and that I'd be cured of deafness, but no miracle like that ever arrived. Instead, the minister's wife offered a word of prophecy—a prediction of things to come. Mama recalls exactly what was said.

"Derrick will do great things one day," the minister's wife said in prayer over me. "His life is going to touch millions of people for good."

I couldn't tell you for sure today if that's ever come to pass. People say I give hope to a lot of people, and I certainly hope my life touches millions of people for good. That's one of the reasons I talk in schools today, to help encourage kids. There's plenty of people in life who will tell you that you can't do stuff, or that you're not good enough. You feel bad if you think you're alone or you think you're different from everybody. Nobody wants to feel that way, so that's my message: You're not alone. Never give up! If just one of those kids leaves an assembly I'm talking at and he knows that he's not alone in this world, I consider that a success. If you can just touch one person's life for good, then I'm cool with that. Just encourage one person every day. I'll work my way up to the millions. That's what I hope I do. But I'm getting ahead of myself here.

When Mama is asked today about that prophecy, she has stronger opinions than me on this matter, and she believes it's come true indeed. God did not open my ears, no. But he opened up my life. The answered prayer is that God showed us through faith that God will get the job done, and God will choose whoever He chooses to use for His purposes. Even with my hearing impairment, I've been able to do things that people said I could never do.

A deaf kid grows up to be a Super Bowl champion?

Mama will tell you *that's* a miracle.

———

My parents separated again around that time, and I don't remember much about that at all. I didn't want to know any details—that's how I felt. I loved them both, and I was always going to love them both, so I just wanted them to keep those things to themselves. And they pretty much did.

But maybe it affected me more than I knew, especially combined with my hearing issues. Once that year I was staying at my dad's place, and there was a boxing match on TV and I was in my room, playing. For some reason I wanted to go find my dad and ask him something, so I looked and looked but I couldn't find him anywhere. I ran from room to room to room, all the while growing more and more scared. I kept calling to him, and it sort of sounded like he was calling back to me, but maybe my hearing aids were freaking out and I was just imagining things. In my panic, I couldn't quite tell. It wasn't like we lived in a big place, either. It was a standard two-bedroom, one-bath apartment with a front room and a kitchen. Dad wasn't in any of the rooms. While running, I glanced at the bathroom twice, but it was dark.

My mind jumped to a horrifying conclusion: *My dad is missing! I'm all alone!*

Neither of my parents trusted me enough yet to leave me by myself—I wasn't old enough—so my mind reeled with terrible possibilities. Why would my dad leave me by myself? It felt like an intense game of hide-and-seek—all without the fun of being a game. And all the while the volume from this boxing match on TV seemed to grow louder and louder. I kept yelling and yelling for my dad. Suddenly I heard my named called out clearly.

"Derrick!"

I heard that. I wheeled around, and there was Dad. He stood at the doorway to the bathroom with a towel wrapped around him. He was dripping wet. He'd been taking a shower and had switched the light off to stop the fan because he wanted to hear the fight on TV. I couldn't hear the shower running because I couldn't hear that soft a sound.

That was the first time I ever consciously remember being scared of anything—this thought that I was all alone. And maybe these weird things in my ears had something to do with that sense of aloneness. Altogether, I felt strangely unsettled. I didn't like feeling afraid. And I couldn't know it just then, but some of my hardest years were straight ahead, and that was the first time I ever remember feeling like something might be different about me.

It wouldn't be the last.

4

"FOUR EARS"

From the time I was in first grade to the time I was in third grade, my mom lived in Torrance, and me and my brother and sister went to a big school there, Victor Elementary. To a little kid, it seemed like the biggest school ever. There was maybe a thousand kids at the school, mostly whites, but a bit of everything else, too—blacks, Hispanics, Asian. The school itself was this big sprawling brick compound. Outside, blacktop was everywhere. There were a few trees. The hot, blue Los Angeles sky hung overhead.

Torrance was a pretty good neighborhood overall, a nicer place to live than where we'd been in Inglewood. In Torrance, we lived about a mile from the mall, and there was a civic center nearby. You felt comfortable walking down the street or playing outside as a kid. But as nice as that neighborhood was, when I was at Victor

Elementary I played by myself a lot. I don't remember having any friends at school. That was the school, that was the time where I felt out of place a lot, like I was somebody different. I was constantly afraid of what people might say to me—or about me. They had a hopscotch court there, and I played by myself on that. Or I just rode on the swings by myself.

Despite my disability, I always went to regular schools—being mainstreamed, they call it—and even from early on, I was often labeled as "difficult." When a child has special needs, it can often take a while for parents and a school system to figure out how to best handle the situation. The schools I went to had special education programs, but my folks always wanted me in a regular classroom. Looking back, that was good for me, I'd say, although I don't think I met another kid with hearing aids until I was at least in ninth grade.

In first grade, I still had some stomach problems like I'd had when I was a baby, or maybe they got a little worse because of the stress of adjustment. My sister laughs now when she tells of how when I was six, I had this problem where I'd poop the bed. You know how some kids pee the bed? Well, I'd poop it. I didn't have that much control over my bowels yet. Keyon and Tenisha and I all stayed in the same bedroom, and it would get to stinking pretty bad, I guess. They'd try to wake me up, but since I couldn't hear them I'd just keep on sleeping. My brother and sister used to call me "boo-boo boy," because of that. Eventually my bowels got better. We're *all* thankful for that.

First grade is the first time I remember when someone else noticed I wasn't like everybody else. It started when one kid asked,

"Hey, what's that in your ears?" I tried to explain, but they didn't get it or didn't want to listen. That took things to a whole other level. Another kid asked, "How can you *not* hear? That doesn't make sense." You know how if a kid has glasses, others might call him "four eyes"? Well, these guys started calling me "four ears," and began chanting it over and over again.

I don't know if you've ever been there yourself. Standing in a school playground while a bunch of kids quickly form a ring around you. They're all looking and pointing your direction, and shouting the same thing over and over again. You feel pretty miserable. That's for sure.

Ask me today to tell you any more details about that, and I'll tell you, no, I don't remember any more details. That's by choice. It's like this: I tried so hard for so many years to put those details in the back of my head that I never want to bring them up again. Those things happened. I'm done with it. I've worked hard to replace those moments with positive things. And I'd never use what happened back then as an excuse for why I couldn't do something later on. I've taken those details and wiped them out of my head. There's so much for me in life to enjoy today, why would I ever want to remember the bad times? When those things happened, yes, it was rough, but I got it all out then. Whenever I was bullied, I went back to school the next day and continued on. Yes, it was hard. Yes, I felt miserable a lot. But here's what I think: when you come across something hard in life, or if something bad happens to you—and these things definitely happen in life—you can't let your grieving period last too long. There's just too much great stuff out there in the world waiting for you. If you're still mourning something that happened or didn't happen years ago, then you're going to miss out on all the great opportunities that God has placed right on your doorstep today.

Mama stayed strong for me during that dark time in my life. She told me to turn that teasing around. My hearing aids were no different than someone who needed glasses to see. I just needed help hearing. That was all. I tried to focus on that good advice, and it helped develop a same sort of strength within me, but it was no easy road. This name-calling lasted the whole three years I was at Victor. Ages six, seven, and eight. I tried to walk away from it when I could. But sometimes I couldn't, so I'd turn off my hearing aids instead, so I couldn't hear the kids make fun of me. At least I could do that much.

Here's what was going on in my head. Imagine a person's hearing ability being on a scale from zero to ten, with zero being no hearing at all and ten being perfect hearing. Few people find themselves at ten. To have hearing that good is almost abnormal. Most people find themselves anywhere from seven to nine.

With my hearing aids out, I'm at about a two or three. Maybe a one and a half. All I hear is the bass, the deep vibrations at the lower end of the sound scale. Within a person's eardrums, the bones vibrate together very quickly, but mine vibrate far slower than normal. I can't hear higher-pitched noises at all. Female voices are extremely hard to hear. If someone's behind me, and I don't have my hearing aids in, all I hear is mumbling. If you could somehow put on three sets of noise-canceling headphones all at the same time, you'd know about what it feels like for me.

With my hearing aids in, on a good day I'm about a seven on

that scale. But sometimes I'm as low as a five. A hearing aid is basically just a microphone that amplifies sound. It's quite hard for me to be in a roomful of people, because what happens then is that all the noise in the room becomes louder. When I'm with a lot of people, I need to consciously focus on the person who's talking with me. It's a trained-brain response. My brain needs to focus on the source of the sound to hear it clearly. That took a while to learn, and particularly when I was in elementary school, I wasn't all the way there.

I could have learned sign language, but because my parents always wanted me in regular schools, we all quickly concluded that sign language wasn't going to be the answer for me. Who else in a public school knew sign language? Not the teachers. Not the kids. Not my parents or siblings when I was home. Simply put, if I wanted to interact with anybody, then I needed to learn how to talk normally with them.

Fortunately, reading lips came fairly easily to me. And that's primarily what I do on the field today, which I'll talk about a bit more later on in the book. I can hear some sounds, but that's pretty much impossible to do in a noisy stadium, where the sound feels like one continuous roar to me. When you lose one of your senses, then the others have a way of compensating. You can take classes to help you learn to lip-read, but I never did. I just watched people as much as I could, and eventually I started to pick up what they were saying by watching mouths. That ability didn't happen overnight, though.

Part of the isolation I felt came because I didn't want to interact with others. And I didn't want to interact with others because

I didn't know what to expect. At that young age, many of their responses to me weren't positive. In addition to being called "four ears" all the time, I was known on the playground "the kid with the big ears."

Kids made fun of the way I talked, too. When you're hard of hearing, it's really difficult to hear certain letters, like *s* and *r*. If you don't hear a letter, then you can't say it. So with "school," I'd say it "cool." Or with "stop," I'd say it "top." (Of course, if I said "top" when kids were making fun of me, they'd just do it all the more.) I started speech therapy, and gradually that began to help. But still, those years were really hard.

Mama stayed my rock during those years. "Don't ever worry about what people say about you," she told me. "They can't determine how far you will go. Only God can."

I liked that. She was reminding me that better days were ahead. They had to be. They just had to.

With my hearing aids in, I found that I could even use a regular telephone as long as it was set to "speakerphone." But a landline without the ability to be set to "speakerphone" was very difficult for me to use. Landlines actually frightened me. If a landline was put to my ear it felt like a test, one I was surely not going to pass. My grandma had an old rotary phone, one of those ancient circle dialers, and I remember one day at her house she handed me the phone because somebody wanted to say hi. I took one look at that phone and handed it straight back.

I didn't feel angry at the kids who made fun of me. I just felt sadness. Or maybe my feeling was frustration. Whatever the feeling was, it wasn't good. Sure, I tried to talk to them to tell them to stop, but they wouldn't. When they wouldn't stop, I felt so out of control. Something's happening to you and you don't like it, but you can't get it to stop. I developed an aggression from those early experiences of being bullied. That sadness or frustration or whatever it was just got bottled up in me for a long time. I needed to find an outlet—and I needed to find it soon.

———

One day after school when I was in second grade, I was waiting at the park near the school because my sister wasn't there yet, and she would always walk me home from school in those days. Tenisha took some hits, too, for her brother being different. On that day while I was standing there, these older girls came up and started to call me names and accuse me of things. I was seven years old, and they were probably ten or eleven, a lot bigger and taller than me. These girls decided to take the bullying to a whole other level. The group jumped on me and started to punch me and kick me. One of the kids grabbed the hearing aids out of my ears and threw them far into the middle of the field. I struggled to break free, then ran all the way home.

Right about when I reached home, my sister caught up with me, and I told Mom what had happened. If I talk without my hearing aids in, I talk in a deeper voice, and I tend to shout, because I can't gauge the volume correctly. So I was shouting in this deep little-kid voice about all that happened. Mama took us both by the hands and we went back to that field and searched for hours. Finally we found my hearing aids. Mama took us home, dropped us off, then went around to where those bullies lived, knocking on doors, confronting the parents, letting them know their kids couldn't do that anymore.

I got along with some of the kids at Victor. It wasn't all bad. Despite my speech impediment, I tended to talk a lot in class. A social side of me was coming out, fueled by all my adrenaline probably, and most days by then I was just a big ole chatterbox. Whenever I talked, I had this way of getting other kids to start talking, too. So I was deemed the "instigator" and got in trouble a lot for that. I just needed to be active, and if I couldn't move my body, then I needed to move my mouth.

It got to the point where every week I needed to get a progress report filled out by my teacher that I'd bring home to my mama. The teacher graded me on how I'd done throughout the week on three things: attitude, effort, and whether I got all my work done. Getting my work done was never a problem. Good grades always came easy to me. Effort was no problem, either. I always tried hard at whatever I did. But when it came to attitude, well, that's where the too much talking factored in, so the teacher often gave me a "U" for my attitude. The U stood for Unsatisfactory. Mama was never happy when I brought home a progress report with a U on it. That's for sure.

For such infractions, Mama handed out spankings, as did most mothers in our neighborhood. So did my dad. Any other method of disciplining, like a time-out, just wasn't going to do any good for a kid like me. I did some bad things as a kid, sure. I talked back to my parents. I lied about stuff. I stole some stuff from my parents.

I even took something from a corner store once and got caught. At that age you're testing your limits. You're seeing what you can get away with and what's acceptable or not.

Mama thought I was sweet, and I definitely had that sweet side of me, sure. But I could also be a pretty hardheaded kid. I needed strong discipline. You could stand me with my nose in a corner and I'd just think about how much I was going to move around when I was out of it. Or you could tell me to go to my room, and I'd just have fun reading a book. I loved to read, even back then, and I remember reading all the Hardy Boys books over and over again. I read that whole series at least five times. I'm sure my parents stood me in the corner a few times. I'm sure they gave me a few time-outs. But when it came to disciplining me, a spanking was the only thing that ever worked.

I look back now and I'm actually thankful for those spankings. I know they're not too politically correct these days, but I don't care. A kid—in fact *every* kid—will get spanked in life. It's inevitable. He'll either get spanked as a kid for lying or stealing, or he'll get spanked when he's grown-up for lying and stealing—and then he'll get spanked by the police. Either you learn when you're a kid that there are consequences for bad behavior, or you learn it later, when you're an adult. I'd far rather be disciplined as a kid—know what I'm saying? I love the freedoms I can enjoy today as an adult, and those freedoms came in part because of good discipline when I was young.

For a while, Mama worked the graveyard shift every night, then came home to cook us breakfast. We lived in a two-bedroom apartment in Torrance, with Mama in one bedroom and me and my brother and sister in the other bedroom in bunk beds.

One time Mama wasn't home and Keyon was taking the lid off a can of beans. He cut his thumb on the sharp part of the can opener and it started to bleed real bad. It even looked like the muscle had popped out of his thumb. He hollered at me and Tenisha to come over, and we all just stared at it. None of us knew what to do. Then Tenisha had the bright idea of calling 9-1-1, so she did, but then she got scared and hung up before they could talk to her. She did that again, and after a while the authorities came and knocked on our door. My brother got his thumb bandaged and we all got it sorted out in the end.

My dad started moving up the ladder at his job. The company merged with Boeing and Dad eventually became a technical writer and worked his way up to a management position. On the weekends he was always working, always trying to make a better way for us.

Right around then I remember he bought two things—a newer Toyota 4Runner and a four-plex apartment building that he could rent out. The real estate market in Los Angeles was in a slump at the time, and he was able to put less money down on the rental units than he did on that truck. He told me about both transactions in detail, young as I was, and he said, "You just watch these two investments over the years, Derrick. One's going to make me money, and one's going to lose me money. You just watch and learn."

Dad was wise about his money, and sure enough, years later I now know what he meant. That 4Runner he bought in 1996 isn't worth anything today. But those rental units are worth plenty. From the time I was young like that, Dad was always giving me advice—as much as he could—about any and every topic in life, whether he'd learned all his own lessons in that area or not. Money, school, dating, working hard. No, he didn't have life all figured out, and yeah, he made his share of mistakes, but he learned from his mistakes—that much is sure.

I quickly understood that Dad was a man of routines. Every Saturday, whenever I stayed over at his place, he got up and cooked us breakfast, and then we'd head over to the rental to work. We spent all morning sweeping up around the place, taking out trash, making sure the grounds were tidy and clean. Dad was always talking to the residents, making sure everything was on an even keel.

I picked up his work ethic early on. Weekends weren't a time for goofing around. Weekends were a time for work. We had afternoons for fun—life with Dad wasn't all work. But work was wrapped around Dad's backbone. He wanted to hand me that hard work ethic for myself. You don't get anything in this life handed to you for free, he'd tell me. Everything you get—even a gift—you need to work for if you want to keep it; you need to work to learn how to use it or keep it sharp.

Here's a direct quote of something I remember him saying to me: "Don't *get* ready. *Be* ready. If you're getting ready, then you're already late."

Some of these lessons came harder than others. One time my teacher gave me a U and I knew I was going to get whupped when

I got home, so I asked Tenisha if she could try to change it for me to a better grade. Her handwriting was better than mine, and I guess Tenisha's changes looked official, because Mama didn't say a word. I don't exactly know what happened in the meantime, but a day or two later we got a knock on the door. It was the lady from social services, and she asked me about getting whupped and why I was so scared of that happening at home to the point I'd change my school grade. Well, I told the lady that my parents weren't beating me; it was just my way of getting punished. We got that all sorted out, but nobody was happy with me about that, that's for sure.

I think my folks saw this frustration and aggression in me and thought sports might prove a good outlet. I played flag football for about a year in a community league and I liked that just fine, even ran my first touchdown. But the place where we played was too far away to drive to every week, so that ended.

After that I played Little League. This was during second or third grade for me. It was closer to home, but I hated baseball. The game was just too slow. The coaches labeled me as "hyper" because I couldn't quite hear what they were saying, and then I'd act out because I needed to move around. I was just being me. I had all this adrenaline flowing through me and I couldn't sit still no matter if it was in the classroom or on a field. Give me a field and I needed to run around on it. I couldn't just sit on a bench and wait for my turn at bat.

With baseball, I played every position, outfield, infield, and I remember only ever getting one good hit. We were playing T-ball, and I swung with all my might. The ball went to the fence and I got a triple. That was fun, a real rush. But that was the only fun I ever remember having with baseball. In between games we kids all hung out and played tag—that was fun, too. But the games themselves were boring. I hated watching. I loved doing.

When I was in third grade, my mom got married to somebody else and we moved with my new stepdad up to Bakersfield, where he lived. They didn't call me "four ears" in Bakersfield, so that felt like a fresh start of sorts, but I didn't like my new stepdad at all. He was a guard at the prison up there, and I never felt close to him in terms of talking to him or anything else. He had a son, too, and my brother and sister were closer to both of them than I was.

My stepdad knew about my disability, so that never seemed like an issue, but really there was just no connection between us. He'd be wrestling on the floor with his son, but if I came over to play, he'd stop. That didn't really bother me. Not consciously, any-way. I don't know. Maybe these days I don't care. He wasn't my dad, and maybe I felt threatened by someone new who was potentially in that place. I never called him "Dad," I always called him by his first name. He wasn't my dad. I already had one.

My dad, my real dad, got to see us every other week. He still lived in Fullerton, and it was about a three-hour drive from Bakers-field to his place. Mama and Dad arranged it where they'd meet in the middle for the handoff at the Wendy's parking lot just outside the Magic Mountain amusement park in Valencia. We never actu-ally went to Magic Mountain, mind you. We just met in that park-ing lot so Mama and Dad could make the switch.

I don't remember much about Bakersfield, except that I felt lonely a lot of the time. Tenisha remembers one time when we were playing around in the garage, and I got too close to an electrical outlet near the dryer. Some wires were sticking out, and one of them sparked and connected with my hearing aid. It zapped me real good, and that was really painful. They didn't take me to the hospital, but I remember crying a lot. I was eight or nine.

I always felt out of place in Bakersfield. It wasn't because of the city itself, or even because of my mom's new marriage—because I'd felt that way before. I think it was just because a lot of my frustrations were building, these frustrations I'd had over the years of always feeling different, never really having any good friends, always being shuttled from one place to the next.

Even though I was still talkative in class, I didn't like to talk to a person if I didn't know him or her. I was always afraid the name-calling would start again, the teasing, the being pinned down on a field by a group of older kids.

It came as a relief to me when after a while my mama divorced my stepdad and we moved from Bakersfield back to Los Angeles. At first we moved in with Grandma Coleman, until Mama could find us a new place to live. Finally we moved to an apartment in Lawndale by ourselves. It wasn't a bad neighborhood, but it wasn't great.

At first I thought it was cool in Lawndale. There was a family who had a daughter and son about the same age as my sister and me. The boy's name was Dalton, and at first he acted like he was my best friend. He'd come on over, ring the doorbell, and ask if I could come out and play. Or we'd play in the apartment with video games or whatever. I was happy to have a friend.

But we all quickly learned he was not a friend at all. This was the fourth time I've moved in a few years, and I was trying to make new friends and fit in, so I was willing to be a follower then. Dalton and I used to walk to school together at Rogers Elementary, and Dalton would brag to me about how he'd been in trouble already with the law. That sounded cool to me, but I also wasn't sure if I wanted to do those things he was talking about. He was a gang-banger, and I didn't know everything that was involved with being in a gang, but I was intrigued.

One time Dalton was with some of his friends and told me to do something I didn't want to do—leave the complex—and when I dragged my feet his friends started picking on me. See, I was allowed outside to play in the area around the apartment complex, but I wasn't allowed to go into the alley, because Mom needed to be able to walk outside and see me. Dalton and these kids wanted me to go into the alley, but I said no. He didn't like that too much, so he followed me inside my apartment. I just sat on the couch and glared at him, then he came over and started to punch me as hard as he could. I didn't know how to fight back. I'd never been in a real fight. I kicked him off me. Keyon and Tenisha were home, and they heard and ran over and kicked him out of our apartment.

I had a special phone that was hearing aid compatible and had big numbers on it. Someone broke into our apartment and stole my phone, then made the fool mistake of calling our home line, which also rang on another phone in our apartment. Mama answered.

She recognized the voice and told Dalton to have the phone back on the double, or else she'd call the police. He brought it back.

Once after school, I was just hanging around, leaning up against a fence with my legs crossed because I was tired. I guess you don't do that, because Dalton saw this and started making fun of the way I was standing, calling me a girl and stuff. I just ignored him and started walking home by myself, but he ran up behind me, jumped me, and started hitting me again. I dropped my backpack and got loose from him and ran all the way home.

Mama didn't condone fighting. Neither did my dad. At the same time, they always said that they wanted me to stand up for myself. This was something they'd learned from their parents and were passing along to me. If ever I got in a fight, then I was going to get in trouble from them—they made that clear. "If you're in a fight, you'll either get one whupping or two," Mama said. "One will come from me, guaranteed. So you best make sure the other doesn't come from the kid you're fighting against."

When I was in fifth grade, my mama and my dad got back together, so that seemed like a real happy time for everybody. Halfway through the school year, we moved from Lawndale over to Fullerton, where Dad lived in one of the units of the four-plex he owned and rented out to others.

Fullerton is a good, solid family neighborhood in Orange County. Sometimes when people hear you're from L.A. and if you're a person of color, they immediately assume that you grew up in a bad neighborhood. But that's not the case in my upbringing. I lived in a few bad neighborhoods in the L.A. area, but Fullerton wasn't one of them by any means. Cal State Fullerton is nearby, and there's a lot of university people and professionals in the area. It's just a good, basic suburb, but it did prove a bit of a culture shock, moving there from Lawndale. We went from a school where the kids were predominately black and Mexican to a school where there were maybe four black kids in the entire school. As good as Fullerton is overall, it wasn't perfect. I remember getting called the N-word a few times when we first moved there. That was different. I'd come home hurt and Mom would have me sit down at the kitchen table and ask me what was wrong. I'd tell her, and she'd say, "You can't let that bother you. Don't let the negative things in. You gotta stay upbeat and positive."

I took that to heart.

I remember the first time the racial name-calling ever happened, she brought out a dictionary because I wasn't quite sure what the word meant. The N-word wasn't in that particular dictionary, and Mama said, "Okay then. If it's not in there, then it doesn't apply to you, does it? That word is something offensive, and *that's* not in your character, so never let someone else take you out of your character. You are not an ignorant person. Who's being ignorant—you or them? If it's them, then you leave that person alone and don't respond back."

After it happened more than once, I'm pretty sure Mama called the school to intervene, but the school never did anything about it that I can remember. Maybe they said they'd talk to the students, and maybe they did. You never know. Sometimes kids are going to call you names. It's not right, but that's how life works.

As always in a new school, kids wondered what was in my ears, but at this school only one or two kids made fun of me, and not a whole gang of them, so it wasn't too bad. The name-calling may have only been because I was a new kid and not because of my hearing aids.

I told them I could read lips, and most of the kids thought this was cool. They'd say things with only their lips and see if I could figure out what they had said. Usually I could. But one time this kid came up to me and whispered, "I love you," then gave me a smirk and asked if I knew what he said. I'm like, "What are you trying to say, man?"

"Olive juice," he said with a shrug. It was just a joke, and he knew it. I tried it out myself. It was true—my lips moved exactly the same way with both phrases. Looking back, I don't know for sure if he was mocking me or just having fun, and I don't really care anymore today. But I do remember that the experience made me pay more attention overall to how people talk.

One good thing that my parents instilled in me was not to care if people joked around with me, even though sometimes it might be teasing. "Just don't care about stuff like that," they'd say. That made sense to me. Somebody's always going to be a joker. You can't let it ruin your confidence.

In Fullerton, living with both my mom and dad, I felt stable then. I made a few friends, and I had fun playing outside with a scooter and a skateboard. I always knew my folks loved me—my sense of instability didn't come from them. It usually had to do with my hearing issues and with moving again, but this time it just felt like we weren't going to move, and I really liked the idea of staying put for a time.

In fifth grade I also started working with a new audiologist, named Nancy Adzovich, and she was well versed in everything I needed. She laid out a plan for the next few years and held everything to a higher standard.

Still, I felt adrenaline coursing through my veins. When I was in sixth grade, Tenisha started being a cheerleader for the boys' football team. I hung out and watched the games, and that looked pretty cool to me. Football—not flag football, but real football. Tackle football. The way all those guys were charging up and down the field like that. I could picture myself doing the same.

They only question now was if they were going to let a kid with hearing aids play.

5

FOOTBALL, BASKETBALL, OR A LIFE OF CRIME?

And the answer was *No, they weren't.*

Tenisha cheered for the Fullerton Wolverines football team, and Dad and I often went to watch them play. It's hard to describe what I first felt toward football. I wanted to play badly, and I knew if I got the chance to play then I would give everything I had to the game. But I also loved basketball—in fact, back then I loved basketball even more than football. So there was this side of me that sort of shrugged at first and said, Well, if I'm not allowed to play football, then that won't be the end of the world. But I still wanted to play football.

My dad brought the question of whether or not I should play to my mom. Dad had played football back when he was in high school, and he knew how rough the game can get. I've asked them about that early conversation, and basically my dad said to my mom, "Derrick Jr. is sort of interested in playing football. But I don't think it's a good idea. What are your thoughts?" And Mom agreed with Dad. When I talked to my mom about it, she was pretty strong about it and had all these questions for me that I knew I wasn't supposed to answer back. "Are you going to get a head trauma? Are you going to lose your hearing aids? How's that going to work out for you?"

So that was sixth grade, and the answer was final.

In sixth grade they didn't let me play.

Despite that, sixth grade as a whole went pretty good. Way better than earlier grades. I wasn't getting teased much, and I quickly developed a reputation as a good athlete, so that offered me credibility on the playground.

How it first happened was we had a school field day in sixth grade where we did all sorts of running races, the hundred-yard dash, the long jump, that kind of thing, and I won one blue ribbon after another. My folks and I knew I had some athletic abilities, but none of us knew exactly how much. After that field day, kids in school started acting like I wasn't just the deaf kid anymore. I had a bunch of friends almost immediately. My mom and dad took note that they needed to channel all that energy and raw talent into organized sports.

I remember in particular two friends from sixth grade—Adam and Amanda. Adam was in the same grade as me but at least a year older than everybody else, because he'd started late. He was Hispanic, and you could sense that he felt out of place as an older guy in a younger grade, so maybe that shared feeling of being out of place initially drew us together. We could both relate to feeling that way. Adam was a bigger guy, strong and athletic. He looked like he was about fifteen. I think he was even shaving back then, and we were always competing against each other, sometimes in PE class, or just at lunch or recess. Sometimes it was who was better in soccer, or who could hang from the monkey bars longer.

My other good friend, Amanda, was a basketball player. She was that girl growing up who was always so good at sports, she played on the boys' team. We hung out shooting hoops. She was tall and lean, a tomboy, not a girly-girl at all, and always hanging out with the guys. Eventually she grew up and became a beautiful young woman and played for Long Beach State. She's one of my best friends today.

It felt good to have at least two kids who I felt safe with. The three of us had other friends, too, but with Amanda and Adam, I could be myself. The love for sports connected us, and maybe even the subconscious feeling that all of us were just a bit different: Amanda was strong and played on a boys' team. Adam was older than everybody else in our grade. I needed to work hard to make sure my disability never held me back.

Ultimately, it didn't matter what connected us. With Amanda and Adam as my friends, it felt like those bad days were over, those brutal days in elementary school where kids made circles around me and called me names. But there were other challenges ahead.

As I've mentioned, I could be pretty hyper as a kid. Always active. Always moving around. Even a bit reckless. I had a ton of energy. When you're a kid, sometimes you put that to good use, sometimes you don't. My behavior wasn't bad, but I'm sure I enjoyed irritating my siblings from time to time. My parents sometimes, too. I always wanted to be doing something. My dad put me in tennis, and I liked that. My parents also put me in basketball in a community league, and I loved that.

A year went by and I asked my folks again about playing football. This time they thought about it more. They knew that sports as a whole were good for a growing boy, particularly one as active as me, so if I was still interested in football, then maybe at least they should check things out.

Mama took me to the pediatrician, explained the situation, and asked what she thought. The big question was if getting hit would do any damage to my bone structure. If my structure was in any danger by getting tackled in football, then that could cause more hearing problems. Nobody wanted that.

The doctor ordered an MRI. If you've never seen an MRI machine up close, it's this huge tube that you lie in, and you need to lie perfectly still while it takes pictures of all your insides. It wasn't easy for me to lie still for that long. I wasn't scared. I was just bored. You just lie there and lie there and lie there, and that's all you do. If I'm ever lying down, I don't like to just hang out with my thoughts. I like to be doing something—playing a video game, watching TV, or reading a book. But things worked out, and the

MRI showed that my skeletal structure would take the hits of football fine. So Mama signed me up, just like that, and at the start of seventh grade I was playing football.

Whenever my parents did something for me, they did it wholeheartedly, and my playing Pop Warner proved no exception. When asked today about the amount of work it took and why they put in all that work, they say they thought football might give me that additional outlet for my energy, which would be good for me. Maybe football was even what I was born to do. Mama describes me back then as "tough and rough and sometimes a bit hyper," so it made sense for me to get out there, get my energy out, and see what I could do.

Dad talks about how most parents are invested in their kids, and he and my mama were no exception. They wanted to make sure I was supported in football, and if I had the chance of becoming exceptional, then that was certainly something they wanted to nurture. Every family needs to do something together, and football fit the personality and temperament of ours. It set the tone. It was something that needed to be done. So we pulled together and did it.

Pop Warner football is a big community league named after its founder, Glenn Scobey "Pop" Warner, who coached college football for decades in the early twentieth century. The organization is huge, all over the United States, and they've even got some leagues overseas now. They've also got Pop Warner cheerleading and Pop Warner dance squads. You can be anywhere from ages five to sixteen to participate in the organization, and you've got to keep your grades up or else you can't play. They also have weight requirements for each of their eight divisions of football, the idea being that if you're some 85-pound ten-year-old playing Junior Midget, then you won't get pulverized by some 185-pound fourteen-year-old. Makes sense.

As an eleven-year-old seventh grader (I'd turn twelve that October 18), I started out in the Junior Midget division, where kids can be anywhere from ten to thirteen years old and weigh anything from 85 to 145 pounds. I could have played the next division up, Midgets, but kids can be as old as fifteen in Midgets, and Mama didn't think that would be good for me. There can be a lot of physical and mental difference between a fifteen-year-old and a twelve-year-old. Plus, some kids in Pop Warner had played football since they were Tiny Mites, so they knew the sport a whole lot better than I did. Mama and Dad both agreed that it would be best to play at the division level where I was supposed to play.

There was only one problem.

Already by age eleven, I was about five foot eight inches tall and weighed just under 145 pounds. I was a muscular kid and still growing. I mean, thanks to my size, I was right up against the threshold of needing to be bumped up to the bigger division. I think I was 143 when I first weighed in for Pop Warner—and there wasn't an ounce of fat on me. The cutoff was 145 pounds. If I wanted to play football—and I did—then I needed to keep my weight right where it was. You know how hard that is for an active, growing boy who loves to eat?

Muscle weighs a lot, so I could keep what I had, but I couldn't bulk up at all. I started going to the gym three times a week with my dad, although never to lift any heavy weights. We warmed up by running a mile on the treadmill at a good speed. Then I did sit-ups, push-ups, abs, and dips. Sometimes I'd do bench presses using the weight bar but no weights. Or I'd do leg presses with no weights on the machine. I always did calf raises, because I was always hopeful my calves would get so strong that someday I could dunk in basketball.

I did workouts at home, too—same exercises as I did at the gym, along with the addition of bear crawls in the front yard. Have you ever done a bear crawl? I hated bear crawls then, and I still hate them today. This is where you propel yourself for as far as you can go on all fours without allowing your knees to touch the ground. Bear crawls have been a favorite exercise of pain-inflicting football coaches and military drill sergeants for years. Your chest and shoulders just kill afterward. If I ever got in trouble with my dad, he'd make me do bear crawls as a punishment. Sometimes I did them anyway. They hurt, but I knew they were good for me.

I also started to run all the time, trying to get myself lean while keeping fit. Near our house was a hill where I could run a three-mile loop up and down and around that hill. Some days I ran that loop three times—once in the morning, once in the afternoon, and once late in the evening after homework was done—just trying to kill the water weight. Sometimes I ran with my dad or mom, sometimes I ran by myself. We timed me so I could get faster. Dad lost twenty pounds from running with me so often. Football is a marathon, and if you have good lungs and great strength, then you can usually do okay for the duration of a sixty-minute game. It might seem like football players are resting when they're just milling around during plays, but that isn't the case. You're always on the go.

At football practice, we always began by running a lap around the field to warm up. We shared the field with the softball teams, so we needed to run around all the backstops. The run might have been a warm-up only, but it always turned into a contest to see who could finish first. When I first started football, I typically finished mid-pack. But after I started running like that all the time, I consistently finished in the top five.

My mom only bought healthy breakfast cereals for me to eat. Every morning, I ate Kashi GOLEAN with strawberries. All my food was organic. Everything was measured. We monitored calories every day. We weighed me every day. For lunches and dinners, I ate every combination of salad you can imagine. I ate salad with barbecue sauce, salad with hot sauce, salad with a little bit of chicken in it. Mom took all the junk food out of the house and kept it in the trunk of her car. Usually I toed the line, but sometimes at school, I'd get so hungry that I'd cheat and bum a bag of Cheetos off a friend. Sometimes for a snack, when I couldn't find anything in the house, I ate uncooked spaghetti noodles.

As a rule, I love to eat. Before football started, if Mom brought home a box of Twinkies from the store, I could eat that whole box in ten minutes. I particularly loved anything sweet. I still do, and it's going to cost me my teeth someday, I just know it. I also love meat. These days, I'll go to a steak house, order the biggest porterhouse they've got, and kill it in no time flat. My older brother was always tall and skinny, and he ate more than anybody in the family without gaining an ounce, but that never worked for me.

There were times when I didn't want to run, but I'd step on the scale and be 146 pounds, so I'd go run anyway. On game days, I never ate before weigh-in, and I'd weigh in wearing just shorts. Thankfully, I never missed a game because of my weight. The coaches used to make an example of me to other players, if any of them were having problems with their weight. They'd say, "Coleman can make weight. You guys have no excuses." If a guy didn't make weight at practice, then he needed to spend all practice running.

People would ask me, "Why you doing this to yourself?" It seemed crazy. But I knew why I was doing it. If I was going to play football, then I wasn't going to play it halfheartedly. If you're going to do something, then you gotta do it with all you've got. Sure, at that point in my life, I may have even loved basketball more than football, but I wasn't putting this kind of energy into basketball. It just didn't require as much.

It was a good thing that drive burned within me, because when I first started playing football, I wasn't very good. My dad says I was average, but I think I just plain sucked. The problem wasn't my athleticism. I could run and sprint and throw and catch. But I didn't know anything about football. That was one of the big reasons I needed to push so hard.

In football, basically there are power moves and finesse moves. For some moves, you just need brute force. But for other moves, like how to evade a potential tackler, you need to be nimble. For example, if you're on offense and the ball is snapped, then you need to very quickly determine which player is going to try to tackle you, and that could be more than one guy. You can be sure the guys coming against you are using their body and hands and all kinds of tactics to shed a block and get you tackled. In addition to that, it took me about two years to figure out the hitting. At the beginning I wasn't protecting myself, and a coach won't let you play a lot if he thinks you're going to get hurt. Another thing I was doing wrong was hesitating until a player came to me. The natural tendency to hit someone is not there in most people. When you hesitate, you've already lost the battle. Dad would sit me down and say, "Hey, you need to make first contact." This is something you need to mentally train yourself to do. So I started making first contact. Plus, I was still learning balance. When you're hearing impaired, sometimes it takes a while to learn how to listen to the equilibrium in your ears. Whenever I played basketball, I tripped and fell a lot. So eventually I learned how to balance better.

And then there were the hearing aids.

We quickly learned that there were three problems with those: the fit of the helmet against the devices, the movement of the hearing aids inside my ears whenever I ran or took a hit, and the screaming in my ears from feedback.

The helmet issue was a fairly easy fix. We changed the jaw pad so it wasn't as thick, and everything worked off that. A jaw pad is connected to the helmet by three points, so I'd disconnect two points and I could wiggle my helmet off without taking my hearing aids out. Even that took a bit of doing, and I never took my helmet off during practice, even when it was hot.

The feedback was caused mostly from the hearing aids being loose in my ears. If ever the hearing aids are loose, then I hear a squealing sound, which can get really loud. If something gets close to the hearing aids, then they have a tendency to scream. Once my helmet was tight, my hearing aids didn't scream.

Keeping the hearing aids from falling out proved the biggest obstacle to overcome. We tried everything to fix it. And I mean everything. I wore headbands in basketball—and that worked for that sport. But we needed something tighter for football. At first we tried a selection of various headbands—different brands, different materials. We tried bandanas. We tried hair scarfs. We tried a terry-cloth towel. I was always walking around with all kinds of stuff on my head. My dad went on websites and talked to helmet and hearing aid manufactures, always trying to find something that would work. But nothing did.

Finally, one day my mom was back at the house and got the bright idea to cut up a pair of panty hose. "Derrick—try these!" she shouted to where I was. I came over. She had the top portion of the pantyhose, stuck it on top of my head, and sent me to practice. I came home that day and said the magic words: "They worked fine. They stayed in place. There was no feedback."

From then on, it was a done deal. I was a panty hose man. Times have changed and I use a skullcap today, but I wore panty hose on my head with no complaint for some time. You gotta use what works!

───────

Dad used to take me to big abandoned parking lots and let me drive. When I was really little, he'd sit me on his lap and I'd steer.

When I was older, he allowed me to be behind the wheel on my own, with him in the passenger seat. I remember him teaching me to drive when I was in middle school, and I always liked that about my dad. He was tight when it came to a lot of rules with me, but at the same time he always gave me a fairly long leash in life. He'd give me lectures and show me how to do stuff, then, after that, I needed to figure things out for myself. He always instilled in me that I needed to take responsibility for myself.

My dad and I have always had a close relationship. Me and my mom, too, but with my dad it's different. For a father who didn't live with his son for much of my life, Dad has definitely been there for me during hard times. A few of those hard times I caused myself.

I don't do drugs at all today. I tried marijuana in high school, but the reason I never did drugs was that Dad always told me drugs were stupid. That—and because of the D.A.R.E. program in middle school. That D.A.R.E. program scared the crap out of me. They show you all those pictures of crackheads, and I was looking at them thinking, *Man, there's no way I ever want to live like that.* I had a few family friends who got sidetracked into drugs and I saw what they went through, and I never wanted to venture in that direction.

Nope. Drugs weren't my problem.

That first year I was playing football, I had two friends, Peter and Roger, and I used to hang out with them playing basketball in a big cul-de-sac near some apartment buildings. Mama had always told me not to let others dictate where and how far you will go. But that was some advice I was still not ready to take. Peter and Roger and me rode our bikes everywhere. We loved bike riding. One day it was just Peter and me, and we decided to ride our bikes over to the Brea mall, about twenty minutes away. We rode over and hung out a bit, but there wasn't anything to do and we were bored, so, just being the seventh-grade idiots that we were, we shoplifted a couple of things. Just small stuff, just to see if we could get away with it. A pencil here. A pack of gum there. I'm not innocent in this. Even shoplifting small stuff is wrong.

Now, it's easy when you're shoplifting things to want to take bigger and bigger things. We had a taste of the cake by then, and we were still bored, so that's when Peter had the bright idea of going to try on shoes. Having cool shoes is a big deal to a kid. I'm talking about the right basketball shoes—and these shoes ain't cheap. Peter tried on the coolest pair of shoes he could find, looked at me, and said, "Just put them in the bag." I looked around for security cameras and shook my head, like I didn't want to do it, so Peter took the new shoes to the dressing room, put them on in there, and we both walked out.

We were walking through the mall, wondering if we should go home and feeling that crazy combination of guilty and glee, when all of a sudden I felt this firm hand on my shoulder. I looked over at Peter, and he had a firm hand on his shoulder, too. A deep voice behind us said, "You boys need to come with me." We were caught.

The security guard took us to the office and called our parents. The police were informed, too, and we were charged with misdemeanors. Peter's dad came and got him. My dad came and got me. My dad never yelled at me that I ever remember, but he looked me dead in the eye and told me how it was. I knew I was in deep trouble. What also concerned me was that I had a basketball game later that day, and I really wanted to play in it, but I knew I could kiss that goodbye. I'd be grounded or whupped or both, I wasn't quite sure.

Outside the mall, on the way to my dad's truck, he asked me all these hard questions—What was I thinking? How could I be so stupid? Where was I headed in life? Did I realize how serious this all was?—those kinds of hard questions. He put my bike in the back of the truck and drove me over to the house, but to my surprise he said, "Get your stuff. You're going to the game."

I had a lot of questions too, like, why was I being allowed to have this privilege like this? But I kept my mouth shut, went and got my basketball shoes and uniform, and came back to the truck.

"Get in," Dad said.

I obeyed.

Right before we got to the game, Dad explained himself. "Derrick—you need to take care of three things." His voice was really firm. "You need to take care of your school. You take care of your homework. And you take care of your sports. That's your job: school, homework, and sports. You take care of those three things, and everything else will take care of itself. Understand?"

I was starting to understand. Plenty of other kids my age were making wrong choices, just like Peter and I had just done. They were stealing stuff, or messing with drugs, or messing with the wrong crowd of friends. Those could be my choices if I wanted. I was old enough to be responsible for many of my own decisions. But there was a better life waiting for me if I made the right choice. Dad was telling me that sports were my out. It wasn't like I had a rough upbringing or anything. I wasn't trying to escape a bad neighborhood or even a bad life or isolation. But Dad knew that plenty of things can trap a young man. He was telling me to avoid those traps. Sports are what I love to do, so why would I ever do anything else that takes me away from doing what I love?

It's funny, years later when I got to Seattle, John Glenn, the Seahawks special teams' coach, sat us all down on the first day and basically said the same thing: "With everything you do, you need to put your best effort and best attitude toward it. Those are the things you can control—effort and attitude. If you write a paper, if you do a job, if you're playing sports, there's a high probability you're going to succeed if you put those two best things forward."

I was listening that day in my dad's truck. I made some mistakes after that, but I never strayed for too long. Staying the course was my dad's philosophy. That was the coach's philosophy. And over time, that became my philosophy, too. I've never been sorry I chose the right path.

Middle school was sports, sports, sports. I was always going somewhere, to a game, to a practice. I played football in the fall, basketball in the winter, and baseball in the spring. Summers, I'd play community leagues—as many sports as I could. Sometimes two sports would overlap, and I'd be changing from one uniform into another in the car on the way over to a practice. I was always in a uniform.

I liked that. It worked for me. And I'm going to do similarly someday when I have kids—always keep them playing some kind of sport. Sports became the venue where I channeled all my energy—and I had a lot of energy to channel. Sports were social, too. Some people connect over schoolwork or in a club, but I connected by playing sports. When I played sports I felt like I was doing something important. When I played sports, I didn't feel different from anybody else.

I could be an aggressive, high-energy kid in those years, and in basketball I was always fouling out because I played too aggressive. Hey, when I was just a toddler, sometimes my mom needed to put me on a leash at the grocery store so I wouldn't run off. But in football, I found that somehow the aggression was applauded. I could charge as hard as I wanted to. I was commended for my aggression, even respected for it. There were older kids than me on the team, and there were kids who had been playing football longer than me, but I had this relentless drive that I didn't see much in others that age. I wanted to be the best. Whenever I saw a kid better than me, I never felt insecure. I felt motivated. Seeing a kid better than me only made me work harder.

When I first started playing, one of the coaches asked me what position I wanted to play, and right away I said quarterback. Truth was, that was the only position I knew. I'd see it on TV—the guy with the ball. So the coach kind of shrugged and said okay, and he had me start off doing quarterback things. But after two weeks, we all knew that being a quarterback wasn't for me. A quarterback needs to have this inborn ability to size up a field, see what everybody's doing at once, and make split decisions that affect a whole team. That wasn't me. I had an arm. I could throw. That wasn't the problem. In fact, I still have an arm today. I mean, I don't have an arm like Russell Wilson's got an arm, but I'll still go out while we're warming up, grab somebody, and throw fifty-yard passes without straining at all. The problem back in Pop Warner was that I didn't have the right sense of anticipation. I threw the ball toward where a receiver was, not to where he was going to be.

So I moved to tight end, and that suited me better. To play tight end, you need to be a big, athletic lineman who can act as a wide receiver, too. On running plays, you need to be able to block. Then on passing plays, you need to be able to go on a route, depending on what the play is. I found that I liked tight end. The position grew on me. Over time, I made some good catches in Pop Warner. I even made one or two touchdowns. I was on my way forward, and that felt just fine.

———

Off the field, school was mainly okay for me. In seventh and eighth grades I attended Ladera Vista Junior High in Fullerton, and I liked the school just fine. The only problem was that in middle school I needed to start wearing what's called a personal, portable "FM system" to class. With an FM system, you have a wire that you connect to your hearing aids, and a box that acts as a receiver that you wear on your belt or around your neck, whatever you like. Then there's a microphone that you need to give to whoever's up front speaking. In my case, the teacher. Whatever the teacher says is broadcast through the microphone back to the receiver, so you can hear it clearly through your ears. I felt embarrassed about needing to do that.

See, each year I had six teachers in middle school, so I needed to carry this big boxy thing around with me everywhere I went, then walk up to each teacher at the start of class and ask them to plug in. After class I had to go up and collect the microphone and go to the next teacher. Everybody saw me do that, everywhere I went. It was particularly hard for me in sixth grade, because I didn't want to be different like that, even if the FM system made it so I could hear the teacher.

The FM system was actually owned by the school district, not by us personally, so I needed to turn it in to the school at the end of each day, then collect it again each morning. One time we had a family vacation planned to Hawaii. Man, I was so excited about that trip. When the bell rang for school to be over, I just grabbed all my stuff and took off out of there. We were at the airport by the time I realized I'd taken the FM system with me. I was so nervous, but there was no way I was going to say anything about the system now—maybe it would mean I couldn't go on the trip. I felt bad about it, but it wasn't until we had landed in Hawaii that the truth came out. Mom phoned the district offices and explained the situation, and of course it all worked out way better than I'd feared.

By the time I got to eighth grade, I grew more comfortable with the FM system. The technology had improved a bit since two years earlier, and by then I didn't really care anymore. I figured it was helping me, so I was going to use it. Period.

I had a history teacher, Ms. Smith, who was hard on me in

middle school. It was just ridiculous. At first I thought she was going to fail me. She called my mother and said, "Derrick is a smart kid. But he won't be able to fly by in my class. He'll need to work for it." Eventually I started to think that Ms. Smith knew what she was talking about, and maybe it wasn't so bad after all that she was being so strict. So I buckled down, hit the books, and gave it my all. Ms. Smith spent extra time with me, helping me learn what I needed to. I started to really enjoy history and all the politics that surround all those big events and decisions in years past. Years later, in college, I took a lot of history classes and even became a political science major because I enjoyed it so much. That was all thanks to my middle school teacher Ms. Smith.

If I ever had a free moment, I was outside playing sports, usually basketball. When I was playing sports, I felt like a normal kid. At school, at the end of every bell, I'd be outside shooting hoops or playing pickup ball. We'd push it to the limit and go over. Sometimes we'd even take a punishment because the bell would ring but we'd want to finish our game. We'd go to class sweating like crazy.

One day in junior high I met this kid named Derek M. He was half Irish, half Japanese, a tall kid who honestly looked a little weird. We had classes next to each other and needed to line up outside the class while waiting for the teacher to let us in the classroom. While waiting in line, we both said, almost all at once, "Enough of this," and started to chase each other around campus. We were both late to class. We thought the running around was hilarious, and we both became fast friends, mostly because we were both a little weird. Years later, he's still one of my closest friends.

I wasn't paying attention to girls much in those days. I liked a girl named Olivia, but I found it hard to talk to her in middle school. In ninth grade, as a high school freshman, I struck up the nerve to ask her to homecoming and she said yes. It took a whole lot for me to ask her out. After homecoming, I asked her to be my girlfriend, and she said yes. So I felt pretty good about that.

Toward the end of middle school, my parents weren't getting along too well. Tenisha and Keyon and I knew something was coming. Our folks were arguing more. One or the other was sleeping on the couch more. One day they got in an argument about some furniture or something. Afterward, my mom pulled me outside in the garage and said, "Me and your dad are splitting up again." And I was like, "Okay." I already knew what it was like for them to be separated, so I was thinking, *Okay, it didn't work out.* I liked having them live together, but if it wasn't working out, then that's what it was.

A day later, my dad sat me down. I thought I was going to get lectured for something, but instead he asked, "You know your mom and I are splitting up?"

"Yeah," I said.

And he said, "You want to know why?"

"No. That's your business. Not mine," I told him matter-of-factly.

Sometimes when parents split up, a kid will blame himself, but I never did that. This may sound coldhearted, but I'd spent a lot of years with them not being together, so I was used to that already. I knew it could work with the being apart. Sure, I liked it when they were together, but I also knew that I couldn't control that.

My biggest concern was where we were going to live. I didn't want to move again. Not then. Not ever. I'd finally found a school where I had some friends, and I didn't want to leave that. I was scared that maybe we'd move to another school where things would be like they were for me back in elementary school.

My mom started looking in other places in the city, but I got really firm with her—as firm as a middle school kid can get with his mother. We had some words, and I pleaded with her, "This is the first time I got friends. We can't move far away. You gotta realize this." And finally she did. She started looking around the same neighborhood as we were living in, and she found a place just around the corner from my dad's. It was only about a block away. Dad stayed put, and the rest of us moved. I had a big ole basketball goalpost in my current driveway and I literally leaned it over on its side and dragged it down the street to my new house.

I was glad that basketball goalpost came along easily. High school was just starting and basketball was still my main sport. I wasn't even sure I'd continue in football at a high school level. In my junior high yearbook it says, "Most likely to become a professional football player," but I don't know about that. I mean, if you ever saw Derrick Coleman Jr. playing Pop Warner football, there's no way you'd ever say, "That kid is going to play in the NFL someday."

Just before the start of high school, my friend Angelo took me to see the high school freshman football coach. I was still dragging my feet, but the coach didn't even ask me if I wanted to be on the team or not.

"What position you play?" was all he asked.

"Tight end," I said. "But I always wanted to play wide receiver." I said this because I knew I could catch.

"Nah," he said. "You're playing running back."

I nodded.

That was the extent of our conversation. Just like that, I was playing high school football.

Funny how these small conversations have a way of affecting the rest of your life.

6

FROM THE BACK TO THE FRONT OF THE LINE

One of the biggest questions people ask me about playing football and being hearing impaired is how can I hear what's happening during practices or games. A lot of verbal communication takes place during football. A quarterback will call plays in the huddle. A coach will yell things to players when they're on the sidelines or on the field. A good football player is always aware of his surroundings—both what he sees and hears.

When I first started playing football in middle school, my parents made sure the coaches knew about my condition. High school was the same way. Coach Jim Burton (everybody called him Coach Jimbo) was the head coach, and he and his staff were always so loud that I could hear them okay with my hearing aids in. When we players were in the huddle, we were all so young and everybody yelled so loud that I could almost always catch what was being said.

When we were on the line of scrimmage getting set for the ball to be hiked, depending on how much noise was going on around me, sometimes I could hear the snap count and sometimes I couldn't. To compensate, I learned how to watch closely and move the split second I saw the ball move. I never jumped offside or missed a cue. Sometimes a quarterback will change a play when he gets to the line of scrimmage by calling out an audible, and this had the potential to be a problem for me. But I learned to read a situation just like a quarterback does.

Ninth grade, the beginning of high school, was when I needed to really concentrate and start reading lips in the huddle. I was getting more time on the field then, and the play as a whole felt more serious. The quarterback was always filled in, and he made sure to look at me so I could see his lips move. Sometimes I'd need to catch a quarterback to make sure he looked at me, but usually it was never a problem.

We went to doctors on and off in those years, and I was always working with my audiologist to keep improving my speech patterns. Somewhere around the start of high school doctors figured out the reason I'd gone deaf in the first place. The structure of my ears was normal, but I went deaf was because I was missing a hearing gene. Actually, both my parents were missing a gene each, and the combination added up in me.

I think my parents have felt some guilt about that, but I don't fault them in any way. There's nothing they could do about it. Overall, we felt reassured. For years we'd wondered if I'd had some sort of disease that caused the hearing loss, or if it could ever be reversed. The answers now were no and no, so there was a sense of closure that came with that. It was a part of the journey to finally know what had caused the impairment. Nothing else was wrong with me, and things weren't going to get worse.

It was time now for me to start making my mark.

In ninth grade, I started a new school at Troy High School in Fullerton. It was a good high school with a strong sports program, although the athletic shed was kinda old and rickety. Teachers made you work hard in the classroom, too. If you played sports at Troy, then you needed to do well in academics, and my grades were always high at Troy.

Playing freshman football felt different than playing at the middle school level. I was playing a different position—two of them actually—running back on offense, and also linebacker on defense. Overall, I had more confidence about football by then. I sort of sucked during middle school because I was still learning the game in so many ways, but during those earlier years I'd always been willing to work harder—like how I gave extra effort to keep my weight down—and the hard work all started to pay off when I got to high school.

Playing both offense and defense in high school proved a unique training ground for me. A running back is designed to receive the football from the quarterback, mainly as a handoff, and then run through the defensive players to get yardage or a touchdown. A linebacker usually lines up about four yards back from the line of scrimmage. His main goal is to tackle the quarterback or running back, depending on who has the ball. So, because I played both positions, I learned the tendencies of how a player moves in both positions. When I played offense, I learned how to evade linebackers. When I played defense, I learned how to bring down running backs. That helped me become a better player later on.

In high school I got in early with a great group of friends, and that helped a lot. Having good friends is so important during high school. Who you hang around with can affect everything else that happens during those years. Our team's quarterback, Tyler, became a good friend. He was energetic and always positive, a great Christian young man. His cousin, Josh, played wide receiver, and he became a great friend, too. Both of their dads were pastors of churches near the high school. So Tyler and Josh grew up with a deep faith in them and they carried that strong spirit onto the field. Tyler always had the pastor in him, he was destined to follow his father's footsteps, and pastors in Southern California are loud as a rule. So with Tyler being quarterback, and Tyler being loud, that helped me play the best that I could. I'd say my freshman year was one of my favorite years ever. We all had a lot of fun together. The focus was on the journey, not the destination.

And, oh man, once I got to high school I could start eating again. The weight requirements of Pop Warner didn't exist for me anymore, and I just started packing in the food. I couldn't wait to start eating again, and I almost missed the last game of my eighth grade season because I couldn't wait for the game to be over. Right after that game ended, I started eating everything in sight. For days, weeks, months on end, I ate mac and cheese, yams, chicken, hamburgers, mashed potatoes, french fries, every vegetable in sight, every dessert Mom ever brought home. I could polish off a whole bag of Snicker bars at one sitting. I'm all about the sweet stuff, and I love side dishes. Even if I go to a restaurant now, I'll eat my sides first.

I need to publicly apologize to my sister, Tenisha, because if she ever bought anything for herself, then she needed to hide it in her room so I wouldn't devour it. One time I found doughnuts in her closet and I ate the whole box. Another time she bought an ice cream cake just for fun and hid it in the deep freezer. I found it, took a piece, then accidentally dropped the rest on the floor. Sorry, Tenisha.

At the end of my eighth-grade football season, my weight was still under the line at 145 pounds. Eight months later, at the start of my ninth grade season, I weighed 185. My teammates nicknamed me "the Monster," and I kept eating and lifting, eating and lifting, all the time. Kids from other teams were wanting to check my birth certificate, wondering if I was really a freshman or not.

My sophomore year I weighed 195 pounds, almost 200. My junior year I was up to 210. My senior year I was six feet tall, still growing, and topped the scales at a solid 220. I was still filling in my frame, making up for starving myself for those two years in middle school.

I kept running up and down the hill by our house, but not as much. I was already strong because of the foundation I'd built. In ninth grade I started lifting heavier weights to add muscle. Dad kept training me. We didn't do anything fancy. All our workouts were old-school Olympic workouts—bench presses, smashes, clean and jerks, squats. We believed in good shoulders, good back, good core, good legs. By the time I was a senior, maybe even a junior, I could clean-and-jerk 295 pounds and bench-press 310. I wasn't slowing down for anything.

I remember well the very first high school football game I ever played in ninth grade. It was against the Westminster Lions, known by their motto as "Home of scholars and champions." I was playing running back for the first time and I really let loose, but I still didn't know what I was doing. Whenever I got the ball I just took it and ran as fast as I could. I had a couple of fumbles in that game. I was still holding the football wrong, palming it like a basketball, completely unprotected. I had nowhere to go but up.

The linebacker coach, Coach Thomas, was also our school's wrestling coach, and he helped me make necessary adjustments. He was a big, hard-nosed dude, but lots of fun, always joking around. He'd head-butt you just to show you how tough he was and say, "I just hate the sight of blood." Or maybe it was to show you that you needed to be tough.

As the year wore on, we began to find our stride as a freshman team. We ran the ball with heavy offense and basically whupped everybody else in the league. In the end, we went 9-1. We should have gone 10-0, but the last game was against a big rival, and in that game I'd say we were more interested in having fun than playing hard. I rushed a lot that year. I don't know how many yards

I rushed, because nobody kept track at that level like they do now, but with my strength, speed, and new size, I found could run through other players like they were butter. There was nothing fancy about our play. It was just hand me the ball, and I'd charge down the field. That got the job done.

After football was over for the year, I played basketball, and then ran track in the spring. I sprinted in the 100-meter dash, the 200, and the 4x100 relay. I also did the triple jump, threw discus, and did the shot put. All in all, it was a great year with sports. But I soon found out that life was going to get a lot more difficult.

Any high school football program in the United States is typically divided into three programs. The freshman team is usually composed of just guys in ninth grade. Then there's junior varsity, which is the tenth and eleventh graders, and sometimes a few seniors. Then there's varsity, which is the best players, sometimes eleventh graders, usually seniors. Varsity players tend to have two to three years of high school football experience, and you have to be a very strong player to play at that level.

What happened after our ninth grade year was that me and three other players skipped junior varsity football and went straight to varsity. Me, Tyler, Josh, and our friend Robbie were only tenth graders but we were playing with the big dogs. I think we all felt a bit cocky at being picked for varsity right away. I know I did. Actually, I felt a strange combination of self-assured and scared. Right away the four of us formed a pack: it was us against them. We knew the other older players were going to make us work to get in, and sure enough they did.

I knew this other football player on the varsity team, Brandon, a little bit back then. He was a year older than me, and it was right before the season started when we first met. At first, he thought I was a bigheaded freshman who thought he could walk in and do anything he wanted. Maybe that reputation was earned thanks to the great freshman year we'd just had. But deep in my gut I knew that if I was going to play varsity, I needed to raise the level of my play even more, learn a ton, and give it my all. I felt like I had a lot to prove to the older guys.

One day all the varsity players were working out in the weight room. I still worked out with my dad all the time, so I had my set routines of what I did and when I did them. But the other varsity players didn't know that. I wasn't doing the lifts they were doing— actually, I wasn't doing much of anything at the moment—and they thought I was trying to do my own thing, make my own rules. One of them, this really big offensive lineman named Ethan, got angry and told me to shape up and start lifting weights like I meant it. I just shook my head and went back to doing my own business.

I tell ya—it was like a scene from out of the movies. Ethan ran straight over to me, grabbed me by the shirt, pinned me against the wall, and started chewing me out. I thought he was going to plow me in the face for sure. I was thinking, Boy, you better keep your hands off me, but I kept surprisingly calm and didn't even clench my fists. Fortunately, Brandon quickly walked over and defused the situation. After I was out of Ethan's clutches, Brandon took me aside and said, "Look, if you're going to be in here with the team, then at least lift a dumbbell." I thanked him and explained how I had a different workout routine. We got to be fast friends.

Eventually I got to be pretty good friends with that big lineman, too. You talk to Ethan today about that story, and he explains how he thought I had talent but was wasting it. He just wanted his team—our team—to be the best it could be. I respect that about a guy. It's true, if you've got raw talent, that's good, but it's not good enough. God gave you that talent but you need to add your own initiative to it, too. You need to work to develop your talent if you want to go the distance.

Brandon didn't even realize I was deaf until a few days later. That felt good, different from so many of the experiences I'd had in school in my earlier days. One afternoon, some guys on the team were on my case, poking fun at me about something. It was mostly just trash-talking, but after a while I'd had enough, so I said, "You guys can talk all you want. I'm turning these off." And I switched off my hearing aids. It's an effective trick that I'd used before. Guys can trash-talk about me all they want, but I can't hear anything they say, so it doesn't bother me. Brandon walked up to me later, gave me a quizzical look, and asked a few questions about why I wore hearing aids, and what they were like. I could tell he wasn't being nosy. He genuinely wanted to know. I like that about a guy. If you've ever got questions about me, don't ever hesitate to ask. I'll tell you.

For us new recruits, we had raw talent but not much else, and in our first couple of varsity practices Tyler just kept throwing the ball like crazy, and I kept running up as fast as I could. The hits were harder at the varsity level, the speed of play was raised, and the holes were narrower. Josh and Robbie did well almost right away, but it took a couple practices for us all to settle down. I knew that because I had a disability, even the smallest of slipups could send me packing. My life up to that point had always been about me constantly overcoming obstacles, and I'd learned to use that for my advantage. If I wasn't deaf, then I don't think I would have ever worked so hard. When it came to playing varsity football and staying on the team, I didn't let up for a minute. Pretty soon we started getting respect from the other players. They realized we were going to be an asset to the team.

Then along came game day. Man oh man. In the very first play of our very first game on varsity, I got the ball and fumbled it. Someone plowed into my arm right on the funny bone, and the ball came loose. I shook it off, came back, then fumbled two more times, all in the first half of the game. That made three fumbles total, and we still had a whole other half to play! I'd say it was pretty much the worst start ever. Brandon remembers looking at me and those three fumbles and thinking to himself, *Well, there goes the Coleman story.*

Brandon wasn't the only one noticing my mistakes. When halftime came, Coach pulled me aside and hissed, "I just *dare you* not to fumble the ball anymore." He was dead serious, and it was his way of telling me to shape up quick. I'd underestimated the competition. Varsity was harder than freshman football, and it was way harder than Pop Warner. My dad, a technician and lifelong student of the game, believes my initial problem was that I wasn't running the right way while carrying the ball. When you run naturally, both your arms swing in rhythm. When you run with a football, you need to get used to running with one arm attached to your chest, high and tight. I was still running naturally with the football, making it far easier for the competition to strip away the ball. Sure, I'd played football before. I thought I knew how to run with the ball. But varsity football humbled me fast. I could see in my teammates' faces that I was letting them down.

Fortunately, something clicked during halftime. You can turn off a strong will and you can also turn it on. To turn it on, you need to be passionate about a game. You need to decide to do everything you possibly can. You need to unleash. That strong will came on. I focused harder, gave it my all, and in the second half I didn't have any more fumbles. In fact, I scored three touchdowns. They were convincing runs, too, where I was protecting the ball well and running people over. I knew I needed to show people that I had what it takes to stay at the varsity level. We still lost the game, but at least those touchdowns kept us in the race.

In our second varsity game, I learned a good lesson about perseverance. We were down at the half and I was angry. I fumbled the ball, came back to the sidelines, took my helmet off, and threw it on the ground. (By the time I got to high school, they had a different type of helmet with a different jaw pad that was easier to slide off around my skullcap and hearing aids.)

The coach came over to me and said, "Pick up your helmet, Coleman. Calm down. The game isn't over yet." I remember those words well—they seemed so simple, yet Coach was right. The game wasn't over yet. The second half proved to be one of the hardest games we ever fought. All up until fourth quarter, it was close. Then, right near the end, we rallied back to beat them. Our first victory.

All because we didn't give up.

In high school, when I wasn't playing football, I felt like a normal kid. And I liked that a lot.

I knew firsthand what it was like not to have any friends, so I purposely went out of my way to take the initiative and be friendly to everyone I met in the hallways. Particularly if I saw a kid by himself, or maybe he wasn't well liked or was picked on, then I'd try to talk to him, give him a smile, or say something friendly and upbeat.

I did well off the field, too. Academically, I didn't have any issues, and early on my mom and dad started talking to me about planning to go to college. I didn't have any specific career aspirations in high school. I was mostly that kid who just likes having fun doing whatever he's doing. I liked to talk a lot, and I argued with my mother every now and again about normal teenager stuff, so as time went on I thought I might become a lawyer. I took a drama class, and that was a lot of fun. We played these funny, energetic word and drama games like they do in that improv TV show *Who's Line Is it Anyway?*, and I loved those.

I even took Spanish in high school. At first, the teacher didn't believe I could handle the spoken-word portion of learning another language. I was still having a problem saying a few words in English, much less in Spanish. But "you can't do it" were words I'd long put behind me. I worked even harder to prove the teacher wrong, and ended up with a B in Spanish.

Bastante buena, ¿no?

My favorite subject was math. I liked the precision of it, and I always did well. You ask me today what I'm going to do after football is over, and I'm still not positive. But I know that more school will be in my future. I might go get my law degree, or an MBA. But I'm having so much fun right now in the NFL, I figure I just need to enjoy the present while I can.

Year-round, I always played as many sports as I could in high school, and I played rec leagues during summers. In basketball I played forward, and I loved the game, but the acoustics in any gym are horrible. One of my favorite coaches ever, Dallas Moss, was this big biker-looking dude with huge muscles and long blond hair. He was a real yeller. Yelling didn't help me hear any better in a gym, so we wondered how we could overcome that. Mom wanted me to use my FM system with the coach, the same thing I used with teachers in the classroom. She even needed to get special permission from the district for me to use it, since the district actually owned the equipment, not us. Mom got permission, and we tried the FM system, but it didn't help much in the gym. Plus, it felt weird to be wearing this box with wires on it when I was out on the court. We didn't use it long.

Fortunately, we were able to develop hand signals. One play was called "strong," where either Coach Moss or me would point to a bicep, depending on who needed to know the play. Another play was called "flat," where we held an arm out horizontal. We had about five plays that way. It worked well. My dad was the scorekeeper for all the basketball games, and it was great to have him there. Mom was always cheering in the stands.

I got along well with girls in high school, and in ninth grade at the homecoming dance I started dating Olivia, who I told you about earlier. She was the first girl I ever kissed. We were together about a year and a half, then we broke up, then we got back together our junior year until the end of it. At the beginning of our senior year we weren't clicking as well, so we broke up, but we stayed friends.

Mostly my life revolved around sports and friends. My friends and I played pickup basketball in each other's driveways and rode around the neighborhood on bikes and skateboards. At home I liked watching movies or just relaxing, which didn't happen too often. Every winter, Dad took us skiing, and in high school I was introduced to snowboarding. My friend Brian's parents had a cabin up at Lake Arrowhead, and I went snowboarding with them. At first I spent more time on my butt than anything else, but I learned fast since I'd done a lot of skateboarding as a kid.

One winter weekend we went to the cabin at Arrowhead with a bunch of our friends. We found a big sledding hill with a naturally made jump at the bottom, so of course we needed to try it out. After piling six guys onto a sled, we raced to the bottom and launched into the air. For some reason I was on the bottom of that pile when we landed. My hat flew off. My hearing aids flew out. No one was hurt, but we must have spent twenty minutes searching in the snow for my hearing aids. It was hilarious. Fortunately we found them.

Tyler and Josh both went to a church called Eastside Christian, and they invited me to one of their youth group events. The event was called "Ground Zero," although later it was called "Ignite," and I couldn't quite believe that church could ever be this cool. I went to a different church with my mom all the time, but it was always on Sunday mornings, and we always dressed up—which meant a suit and a button-up shirt for me, and it was almost all black people at the church we went to. I actually liked going to church with my mom, because the pastor there always had good things to say, but it felt more like church for grown-ups.

Church with Tyler and Josh was church for high schoolers. It was held on Thursday nights, right after football practice, and we could wear our regular clothes—jeans and T-shirts. The first time we walked over there, I was feeling funny about how we were dressed, and I whispered to Tyler, "Are we going to change clothes or something when we get to church?"

He just grinned. We walked in, and I saw a foosball table, Ping-Pong table, pool table, and a snack bar with sodas and chips. I was like, "What the heck? This is church?" There was a stage with a full band set up, guitars and drums. A bunch of students were already there, hanging out talking and having fun. For the first thirty minutes or so, everybody just played games and ate. I felt part of the group almost at once.

Then the youth pastor took the stage and formally welcomed us all. He introduced the band, and they took the stage. They were good musicians, kind of alternative music, and the words to the songs were projected up on the wall so you could sing along if you wanted. When the band finished, the youth pastor started to talk. He was the funniest pastor I'd ever heard. He talked like he could've been Dane Cook's twin brother. But he was serious, too, and he talked about God and how great He is and how He cares about us. It stuck in your head, what he said, so I started going there a lot. Looking back now, I'd say it was really good for me—for any kid, for that matter—to be involved in a good church youth program during those formative years. Church has a way of giving a person extra hope, of grounding him solidly in what matters.

One time when I was at church with my mom, the bishop was talking about how a person could feel like he was at the end of the line in life. The bishop brought five people up on the stage and had them all stand in a straight line, one behind the other, so they were all facing the same way to the left. He looked at the person at the very back of the line, addressed the crowd, and said, "It's easy to find yourself at the back of the line like this. You can't get no house. You can't find no spouse. You got no money. You got no hope. But as long as you believe in God, as long as you stay faithful to Him, then He will always be faithful to you."

The bishop then told the line of people to turn around so they were all facing the other direction, and he addressed that same person who'd been at the back of the line. "Look at you now," he said. "And it happened real quick—you're at the front of the line now. That's what can happen with faith. God will never let His creation fail. He may not give you as much as He gives to somebody else, but He will never let you fail."

That illustration stuck with me a long time. For a lot of elementary school, I'd felt like I was at the back of the line. But in high school, that line turned around real quick, and I wasn't at the back of it anymore. About halfway through high school I realized this. For once in my life I was actually a popular kid. People liked me for who I was. They weren't picking on me anymore, weren't calling me names and not letting me hang out with them. I had friends, real friends, and I was going places.

For a kid who once stood at the back of the line, this new direction felt really good.

By talking about church like that, I don't mean to say I was perfect kid. Generally speaking, I was heading in the right direction, but there can be a lot of temptations for a young man growing up in a big city.

One temptation was simply for me to get a swelled head. My football stats started become really good. Overall, I had a strong debut for my varsity year. Then, my junior year, I rushed for 2,340 yards and scored 38 touchdowns, both of which meant I'd set new school records. Those stats made me one of the best athletes in Southern California. I also set school records for the most points scored in a season (232), most touchdowns scored in a game (5), and longest rushing touchdown (90 yards). That year I was named the Freeway League MVP, to the first-team All-CIF SS, and a second-team All-County selection. One newspaper described me as "unstoppable." And plenty of other newspapers started featuring stories about me. Some TV news stories did, too. That felt strange at first, talking to the media all the time. At first I was too cocky, and I didn't know what to do with all the attention, but after a while I relaxed, settled down, and learned to be more humble.

The Troy High School football program had one good year

after another, and as a team we were the talk of the town. One year we had an amazing ride and went undefeated during regular play. The Booster Club bought us matching baseball-style caps that proudly displayed "10 and 0" on the front. We went to the playoffs but lost in the third round to finish our season. Out of thirteen games total we only lost one.

I've always liked cars a lot, and I liked to drive whenever I could. The problem was that I started pushing this privilege when I was only fifteen and didn't have my license yet. I'd take my mom's car and head out without her knowing about it. It wasn't like I was doing anything bad when I was out, maybe just going to the beach or something. But one time I took my mom's car and scraped it up a bit. Eventually the truth came out. She wasn't happy with me, no, she wasn't.

That call from the insurance people slowed me down for only so long. One time when Mom was away, I put towels down on the garage floor next to the wheels of my mom's car so I could align them perfectly when I got back. Then I went for a ride, came back, and parked it without her ever finding out. Sorry, Mom, if you're just finding this out now. I was much younger then, remember.

Along with Tyler and Josh, I became close friends with Brandon and three other guys on the football team, Brian, Josh, and Derek M. I always had a curfew, particularly if I was staying over at my dad's house, but once Dad was asleep I used to sneak out and go hang out with my friends. Again, we weren't getting into trouble. We weren't party kids, and none of us drank. We just wanted to hang out. Derek used to come by after eleven o'clock when my dad was asleep, and I'd sneak out of the house and go meet him down the street by this fire hydrant, which was our point of reference. Derek drove a black Tahoe, and we'd just go hang out at his house.

One time a bunch of us were together and we couldn't figure out what to do. So we went for a drive. Every time we reached an intersection, we flipped a coin. Heads, we turned right. Tails, we turned left. We ended up at Newport Beach, got some burgers, and hung out cracking jokes.

Another time we were out late at night and bought a bunch of fruit at the ninety-nine-cent store. Probably fifty dollars' worth. Someone had a baseball bat, so we started playing baseball with all the fruit out on the street. It was hilarious. The game was called "fruit ball," and you've never seen so much splattered cantaloupe in all your life.

Another time we bought huge blocks of ice, went to a nearby hill, put a tarp down, and slid down the hill on the ice blocks. It was like a huge Southern California slip-and-slide. Totally fun.

My dad started getting wise to my ways, and I needed to figure out new tactics to sneak out of the house. I learned that if I left the bathroom light on, closed the bathroom door, and left my bedroom door slightly ajar, then if Dad got up in the middle of the night and looked in the direction of my bedroom, it would just look like I was using the bathroom. I needed to lock the bathroom door and crawl out the bathroom window to get away with it, and that meant sneaking back in through the bathroom window when I got home. I wasn't positive he was checking on me in the middle of the night, but I wanted to stay safe.

It all worked slick, but one time when I got home, Dad was on to me, because the bathroom window was locked tight. There was no way I could get back in. I was busted, and got grounded big-time. Dad was no fool.

———

By the middle of eleventh grade, I was still living with my mom regularly, but things seemed to be growing tenser between us. One day we got into a real bad argument and Mama basically said, "I've had enough. Get out!"

She meant it, too. Like I've said before, I don't like to relive the details of bad experiences, so I'll just say that I know now that the argument was pretty much my fault. Or at least how I responded to what she was saying to me during the argument—that was definitely my fault. She called my dad, and he came and got me, and I stayed at his house for a couple of days. Mama and Tenisha came over and we all sat around the dining room table to figure things out. Tenisha was one of the first to speak. Basically, living with Mom was too easy for me, Tenisha explained. Mama would let things slide. But Dad was more black-and-white. Either you did things his way or not. Dad kept a tight schedule, and you put things back where you found them.

We all agreed it would be a good idea for me to go live with my dad for a while. It took a lot for my mom to let me go like that. But it was good for me to be under a man's roof. The way I figure it, the only one who can teach a young man how to become a man is a man. And my dad was all about discipline. When he was young, he lived in Gardena for a while, which is near Watts. He'd been in some trouble when he was young and he'd learned from his mistakes.

Things went smoothly at my dad's. I settled down a bit and refocused on school, schoolwork, and sports, just like he always told me to. I still stayed in close contact with my mom. We patched up our differences soon. When it comes to sports, I'm a bit superstitious, so I had this need to be at her house before a game to go through my pregame ritual exactly the same way every time Troy played. I took my shoelaces out of my shoes and washed them along with my pads. Then I wiped my helmet the same careful way. When the rest of my stuff was dry, I put my pads in my bag and my shoelaces back in. They say you're always supposed to get a lot of sleep before a game, but I was always too keyed up to sleep. I'd always stay up late, performing my ritual.

The summer before our senior year, everybody was excited about the possibilities for Troy High School football. It really felt like we were all poised for greatness. I've asked Derek M. about that time, and he described how that summer felt to him, like our last summer as kids. We all just tried to cherish that last summer. There was a lot of pressure on us going into our senior year. A lot of starters were returning. We were ranked high. Everybody was expecting a lot from us—parents, schoolmates, people in the city who we didn't even know. Football was just a game, but at the rate we were going, it seemed like the sky was the limit.

Recruiters were already coming by our school, checking us out. Pete Carroll, who was then the head coach at the University of Southern California, came by our locker room. So did UCLA assistant coach Chuck Bullough. Those two powerhouses were even on our campus the same day, come to think of it.

So, that last summer before we became seniors, we basically just wanted to hang out with our friends and be the teenagers we were. We were kids trapped in adult bodies, and when people got to know us, they saw that we were really just weird goofballs who liked to have fun. When it came to football, sure, we worked our butts off, and we loved playing the game. But we had a larger love, and that was for life itself. What made life so enjoyable for me in high school was my friends. I think we all felt that way. We developed a brotherhood among friends, a closeness that can't quite be described. My family had always been everything to me, and then during high school, my friends became part of my family.

I can't quite tell what that meant to me, having friends that close. Given where I'd come from, and the trouble I'd had being accepted for so many years, it was like a healing of deep wounds. Here's one short example of how cool my friends are. When you're deaf, you need to change the batteries in your hearing aids about twice a week. It's just enough apart so it's easy to forget. I was out with my friends a few times and I needed to make an emergency stop at the store to get batteries. Then one day Derek M. basically stepped in and said, "Okay, Coleman, from here on out, I'm going to keep a spare pair for you, too."

And Derek did. As far back as I can remember in high school, he kept a spare pair at his parents' house. And he put another spare pair in his truck. Just because he cared about me. It wasn't like I was irresponsible—I'd often carry my own spares. But Derek wanted to make sure I never ran out. We're all still friends today, and I think Derek still keeps a spare pair in his truck for me even now. Hey, what kind of friends keep spare hearing aid batteries for you when you're in high school?

My friends. That's who.

I can't begin to thank them enough.

7

I START MAKING MY MARK

At the start of our senior year, Troy was ranked number 2 in the county by the *Orange County Register* newspaper, and number 28 in the entire nation in *Newsweek*'s list of Top 100 High Schools. To say we felt pumped up for football coming into that year is an understatement.

At Troy, we played an up-tempo style of "smashmouth" football, a legitimate sports term that means we ran as much and as hard we could. In smashmouth, a quarterback seldom throws the ball. For most plays, he hands it off to the fullback or tailback. For me as a running back, that meant I saw the ball a lot.

One of our first games in September was against Diamond Bar. They threw everything they had against us, and by halftime we were down by seven points. Our quarterback, Tyler, rallied us all in the locker room. "Keep your heads up," Tyler said. "We've still got a whole half to play."

We hit the field at a run. On the first play, Tyler threw me a pass and I charged hard for daylight—forty-five yards all the way to the end zone. Our kicker converted, and the score was tied.

But Diamond Bar fought hard. We were back and forth all third quarter. Then in the fourth quarter, with just over five minutes to play, they regained the lead by three points. We'd come too far to lose this game. We hit them hard and ended up with a 42–38 victory. I scored three touchdowns in that game.

That victory was characteristic of that year. We played some tough teams, but we never let up the pressure. We won game after game—against Brea Olinda, Buena Park, and Fullerton. La Habra beat us 29–22. They were a strong, respected team and one of our biggest rivals ever. Most games were battles, the score close. But I remember we spanked Sunny Hills, 42–0. We were well on our way to the playoffs, probably even a state championship. There was no better way to go out as seniors.

Then the unthinkable happened.

I don't know all the details today, and they were never explained to us very well as students when the incident happened. But in a nutshell we had this player on our team, a transfer student who we barely knew, who was declared ineligible to play by the California Interscholastic Federation (CIF), the agency that governed football at our level. Because of that ruling, the whole team was penalized. We were disqualified from the playoffs and had to retroactively forfeit several of our wins during the regular season.

Our dream was finished.

It was a letdown for all of us, including the school and the community. A few players showed some negativity, but Tyler and a few others provided real leadership. We didn't want this kid who was disqualified to feel bad. It wasn't his fault. It was the football program's fault as a whole, a case of someone not understanding the rules completely. We had a decision to make. We could sit at home and do nothing. We could protest the ruling and make a stink. We could do something negative to take out our frustration and maybe get into trouble. Or we could do something constructive. In mid-November, we decided to take matters into our own hands.

As the first round of the playoffs started, the La Habra Highlanders, our biggest rival and the school who'd beaten us, was set to kick off against Ocean View. Josh and Tyler, myself, Brandon, Josh L., and Derek M. donned our Troy High School letterman jackets and drove over to the game. A few of us painted our faces. There was a message we wanted to send. We strode up the concrete steps and walked straight for the sidelines. And then we stood.

And cheered for La Habra.

We cheered for our rival, the team that had beaten us. In our minds, it was sportsmanship first. We wanted to support our rival out of kinship for the game. That was the way we went out as seniors—with our heads held high. When life hands you a setback, you don't grovel. You don't sink to a low level. You do what's right and never forget who you are.

A couple of things happened that night at the game as a result.

The local newspaper started to take pictures of us. We weren't there for the attention. But I was glad the newspaper noticed some football players doing something good.

Then the principal from La Habra walked over and shook our hands. He talked to us a bit, and said he was glad we were there.

Then, at the end of the game, the entire starting La Habra lineup walked in a single file and shook hands with us.

La Habra won the game, and we were glad.

That's how our season ended.

———

For any number of high school players, the end of the regular football season means the last time they'll ever play.

But for others, the real work is just beginning.

Coach Jim Burton described me in a newspaper story as "a weapon." He said that if I'd been on a high school Pac 5 team (the California Southern Section's strongest division), they'd be getting me the ball as often as they could. But I was perfectly fine with playing in the Southeast Division for Troy. I'd played with a great team and a strong school, and I'd played with my close friends—that was incredibly important to me. When I graduated from high school in 2008, the end of my football career still felt a long way away.

The attention from college recruiters had begun back in my junior year. For my last two years of high school I figured I'd either go to USC or UCLA. Initially I was leaning toward USC, because they were basically my dream team and I'd always respected their program a lot. Reggie Bush and LenDale White, who both played for USC, were my favorite running backs at the time. Other schools came around, too. I don't remember them all now. We got a lot of letters, I'll say that much. San Diego State gave me a lot of interest. Stanford was another. So did Boise State, Oregon State, Washington State, Utah State. I think basically everybody did from what was then the college football's Pac-10 (it's now the Pac-12). I needed to make a decision soon.

All told, I'd had a great high school football career. I was a three-year varsity starter. I was named team MVP and first-team all-league as a senior. I ran for 5,214 yards in my high school career and had a total of 86 touchdowns. In my senior year alone, I ran for 1,084 yards and scored 19 touchdowns on 230 carries. Plus I'd set those school records I told you about earlier. I could run the 40-yard dash in 4.6 seconds. I'd also lettered in basketball for two years and for three years in track, and I carried a B average for academics. All in all, things looked good.

By the time I graduated in 2008, Rivals.com, a scouting service, ranked me the number 3 football running back prospect in the nation. In California, they ranked me number 1.

ESPN's scouting report praised me for being a "productive fullback . . . [who] flashes potential to be a quality, well-rounded fullback." They rated me as the nation's number 2 fullback.

My parents were actively involved in the recruiting process. We made a DVD that highlighted my play, and my folks sent it to every Division 1 school in California. They were motivated to see me succeed in football. Plus, if I was recruited, that meant a full-ride scholarship.

Sports scholarships at the larger schools have come a long way in the last few decades. If you're recruited today, it means that a university is saying to you: "Hey, you come here and play football for us, and we'll take care of everything else." You go to your classes, sure, and study and write your papers and take your exams. And then before and after classes your job is to eat, breathe, think, dream, and play football. You're not rich as a college player, not by any means. But they handle your tuition and room and board, plus give you a food allowance, your books, and a spending stipend on top of things. You don't want to take a scholarship like that for granted.

As I mentioned, we were leaning toward USC and had any number of conversations with them. I really liked Coach Carroll (and who knew back then that he'd later become head coach of the Seahawks?). I signed up for one-day camps with both USC and UCLA, but when I went to a one-day camp at UCLA, then head coach Karl Dorrell called me over at the end and said, "I can't offer you a scholarship right now, but you'll be getting a call from me later." I wasn't exactly sure what "later" meant, but that very same evening, Coach called with an offer.

So we had a decision to make.

Both schools were good, but there was so much good happening at UCLA that I called them back the next day and committed to them, one of the main reasons being that we thought I'd get more playing time there. USC already had a lot of tailbacks—Joe McKnight, Stafon Johnson, Allen Bradford, and Marc Tyler. UCLA was hungrier for the position I played.

But not long after we accepted, Coach Dorrell got fired from UCLA, so we started thinking about USC again. My mom was leaning more toward USC because we knew the coach there and liked him a lot, and my dad was leaning more toward UCLA, but both of my parents tried to let it be my decision. I knew either way they'd be happy.

It came back to our original thinking. At USC I knew who the coach would be, but they had a lot of running backs, so I could get ignored. At UCLA I liked the educational aspect a lot. USC has good academics, too, but it's hard to top UCLA unless you go to someplace like Stanford or Harvard, and I truly wanted to get the best education I could. Also, even though we didn't know who the head coach was going to be yet at UCLA, we knew the running back coach, Wayne Moses, through a family connection. Plus, at UCLA I'd probably get to play earlier on. And I definitely didn't want to sit on the bench.

I wanted to play.

8

HARD HITS AS A BRUIN

I officially signed on the dotted line to go to UCLA on the first Wednesday of February 2008, during my senior year of high school; that Wednesday is the day most high school athletes traditionally sign on. My parents and I went to a restaurant along with some other high school football players in Southern California and their parents and made it a PR event. The press took some pictures. I wore a suit and tie. It was all good.

It fact, it felt mind-blowing to me. Out of all my immediate family, I was a first-generation college student, at least when it came to going to college immediately following high school. Mom and Dad had both eventually gone to college—Mama at a local college for the nursing program, and Dad at ITT Tech to get more skills for the next step of his job—but neither had gone right out of high school. They'd had kids first, gotten jobs, then gone. The direction I was going in felt new to the whole family.

I couldn't quite believe I was going to go to UCLA, either. UCLA is hard to get into. In the fall of 2008, when I began as a freshman, some 55,000 undergrads had applied that year but only 12,000 had been accepted. Today the number of applicants is even higher—I think it's close to double that—and not many more are getting accepted, either. So, I didn't take my acceptance lightly— not back then, and not today.

The high level of academics is one thing that makes UCLA a big draw to prospective students. The sports are another. Back as a high school senior, I knew that UCLA is one of the greatest schools in the country, and their sports program has a long and prestigious history. I felt honored and humbled to be going to the same school as all those great athletes.

I mean, just think of all the sports legends who have come out of UCLA.

Coach John Wooden tops the list. He was never an athlete at UCLA, but undoubtedly the most famous coach in the school's history.

Basketball legends Kareem Abdul-Jabbar and Bill Walton both played for UCLA.

Jackie Robinson, who broke the color barrier in professional baseball, was a Bruin. Not many people realize this, but Jackie Robinson was actually a multisport champ, the first athlete in UCLA history to letter in four sports: track, basketball, football, and baseball.

Golfers Phil Mickelson and Jack Nicklaus went to UCLA, as did tennis greats Pete Sampras and Jimmy Connors, and volleyball star Karch Kiraly.

Jackie Joyner-Kersee won three gold, one silver, and two bronze Olympic medals in women's heptathlon and long jump. *Sports Illustrated for Women* magazine voted her the Greatest Female Athlete of the twentieth century.

In football, Troy Aikman, Kenny Easley, Jonathan Ogden, and Cade McNown all played for UCLA, as did Ken Norton Jr. (his father was boxing legend Ken Norton Sr.). Ken Norton Jr. is the current linebackers coach for the Seahawks.

That's where I was going, just like them: to UCLA.

I mean—That's! Where! I Was Going!

Toward the end of my senior year of high school, I couldn't wait to get there. I developed a bad case of senioritis. Sure, I loved high school, but I was ready to leave.

Graduation day finally arrived. There was hardly time to have a summer break. UCLA is on the quartered system, and football players were told to report on June 22. Classes wouldn't begin until the fall quarter, but we'd start practicing and working out with the team right away.

Without traffic, UCLA is only about a forty-five-minute drive from my house in Fullerton, which meant I could come home on weekends pretty easily, although I wouldn't have my car at the university at first. I remember well driving up to campus on that first day. Mom and Dad came with me, and a couple of friends helped me move all my stuff. I was supposed to share a room with another

player on the team, but he'd just come down with a case of mono-
nucleosis so he wouldn't show up until a few weeks later, which
meant I had the room all to myself for a while.

We weren't sure about all the stuff I'd need. None of us in the
family had ever lived in a dorm room before. While Mom helped
me arrange my stuff in the room, my dad slipped out to a couple of
stores and picked up some groceries and supplies for me. It's kinda
funny now—I remember specifically that Dad picked up a box of
condoms, too, which made my eyes get wide when I saw it. I wasn't
sleeping around or anything, but I think my parents had in mind
this perception of the kind of shenanigans that can happen when
kids go to college. When I looked at that box, I wasn't sure whether
to laugh or feel awkward, but Mama, always a pragmatist, said,
"Derrick, you're going away to college with no kids, and I want you
coming home with no kids, too. Understood?" Dad added, "That's
all I was thinking, too."

So that was that. Once my folks got me squared away, they
left and went back to Fullerton, and I was left alone. I didn't know
what to do at first, so I ambled over to the room of some other
football players and hung out for a while. I felt nervous at first at
the whole thought of beginning school, because I'd moved around
a lot before and knew how hard it is to make new friends. I wasn't
worried about being teased about being hearing impaired in college, but I wasn't even sure if I wanted very many new friends. I'd
made such great friends from high school days, I was pretty sure
we'd be keeping in touch, even with us all in college now.

Right before school began, my old friend Andrew (years earlier I'd gone to preschool with him) was admitted to the school.

I hadn't seen him in years, but we bonded quickly again and ended up hanging out most of our way through UCLA. That felt good, to have at least one person around who knew me. Friends can be everything when you're living on your own.

———

My football career at UCLA started out rocky.

The coaches at UCLA, including the newly hired head coach, Rick Neuheisel, were already filled in about my hearing condition and how to best handle that, so that was no problem. They just told me to explain to the other teammates how I heard the quarterback on the snap and in the huddle and the whole situation. So I did. After about five minutes of playing, they were like, "Fine with us, no problems with Coleman." Prior to that, whenever I played, I always had an additional talk with the quarterback to tell him to make sure he was looking in my direction in the huddle and not to be alarmed if I came and grabbed him and asked to know what he said. So I did that too at UCLA.

What made things rocky was that on the second or third day of training camp, I started to feel a little throb in my right knee. We weren't even practicing with pads on yet, just helmets, so the hard hitting wasn't a factor. I got an MRI and it turned out I had a torn meniscus. It's a pretty common knee injury that happens by twisting or turning too quickly. This was the first time I'd ever been hurt in all the years I'd played football. I'd had bruises before, but nothing like this.

They needed to scope it out. A few days later I went in for surgery in the morning. They pumped me up with anesthesia and I tried to stay awake as long as I could. I remember yelling just before I passed out, "It's the right leg! My right leg!" For some reason, I thought they were going for the wrong leg. Fortunately, they had it correct.

In the afternoon when that surgery is over, normally a guy with a newly repaired meniscus will head home to rest up. But not me. That same afternoon I went straight to the training facility just across the street from the hospital and started working on rehabilitation, icing my knee, trying to get the swelling down, doing thigh exercises to keep the muscles strong. I didn't use any of the painkillers they gave me. Normally, a guy will spend three days on crutches, but I spent only one. Most meniscus tears take about a month and a half to two months to heal fully, but I came back in three and a half weeks. I knew with this knee surgery I'd be buried near the bottom of the tailback depth chart, but I was highly determined to keep earning my spot on the team. I refused to relent.

Our first game, against Tennessee, was a home game, and things went crazy from the start. Our quarterback threw four interceptions, the game went into overtime, and in the last seconds we ended up winning 27–24 on a 42-yard field goal. I hadn't played. When it was all over, a couple of our running backs were hurt, including starting tailback Kahlil Bell with an ankle injury. So that meant a spot was open.

I didn't think it would be me getting that spot. You have a couple of weeks to decide if you want to redshirt a year (which means you practice with the team but don't play, thereby keeping another year of eligibility), and with my knee surgery I was thinking I'd probably do that. But other plans were in the works.

I'd come in with a couple of other strong running backs, Johnathan Franklin, Chane Moline, and Raymond Carter, who'd redshirted the year before. With Kahlil Bell in the picture, that made five running backs total, and any of the others without injuries would be the natural go-tos for that position. But in our next game, against Brigham Young, the coach told me to go ahead and travel with the team anyway—it was either going to be me or Johnathan who earned the spot. UCLA got spanked 59–0. It was our worst loss in nearly eighty years. Neither Johnathan or I played, but the next week, when we were set to play Arizona at the Rose Bowl in Pasadena, the coach looked at me and said, "You're suiting up, Coleman." And I'm thinking, *Out of all these people, you want me to play?* It was no joke. I was the biggest running back we had. They wanted me.

I remember well the first time I took the field in a college game. It was the Arizona game. I had the jitters, and it felt like everyone was watching. In high school football, maybe a couple thousand people are watching at the most. But in college ball, a whole stadium full of people have their eyeballs on you—that's 50,000 to 80,000 people or more, depending on which stadium you're at.

The first play was whistled down with a false start, but I still ran hard anyway and hit a guy. My mistake. At least my run took some of the jitters out of my system. The next play was my first carry. I can still picture it now: me lined up in the backfield; I got the ball and ran straight ahead three or four yards. That was my big debut. I needed to relax and find my element. But that seemed nowhere to be found. We lost against Arizona, 31–10.

In the military, they call it the "fog of war," when your brain turns to mush and you can't remember what you trained to do. Maybe you're a rifleman, and you're trained to shoot in three-round bursts. Then you get to the battlefield and all that goes out the window—you just spray the enemy with all you got. The same sort of thing can happen when you play sports. You've studied what to do, trained over and over for the play. But then the ball is snapped and your brain turns foggy. That's what was happening with me.

In the next game, against Fresno State, I started well. We all did, actually. I carried nine times for 83 yards. Then, in the fourth quarter, we were down by five when the fog of war hit again. We were near the goal line and I got the ball, lost my grip, and fumbled it big-time. The other team scooped up the ball, and that was essentially the end of our game—thanks to me. We still had something like eight minutes to play, but we couldn't find our stride after that. Fresno State won. I cursed myself for that fumble—I should have had control over the ball. Coach Neuheisel defended me in the press, saying every freshman fumbles the ball, and not to worry, I was going to become a great player; the fumble just came at the wrong time.

Despite those kind words, I was feeling pretty low after that game. I just wanted to go home. I was supposed to call my friends from high school after the game, and we were going to hang out, but I never called. They came and got me anyway—I think Derek M. led the charge—and we spent the entire night hanging out, playing games, doing nothing. I felt like I'd let my team and all of UCLA fandom down. My friends were really there for me that night, and I knew success would come if I could just gain some confidence. The more plays I had, the more confidence I was going to get.

Thankfully, my UCLA teammates were for the most part encouraging after the game in which I'd fumbled. Collectively, the attitude was that we took it as a team loss, not a personal Coleman loss, although one or two players glared in my direction and one or two others let me know that fumbles in a clutch moment like that don't happen—period. In my gut, I wasn't convinced it was a team loss. I knew I still needed to find my stride. I remember thinking, *Oh Lord, what's going on with me?!* I was determined to get my brain back.

Before the next game, I did mental gymnastics, specifically walking myself through what I knew to be true: *This is where I am. This is where I'm going to be for the next four years. Get used to it.* If I wanted to keep playing at UCLA, then I needed to overcome the fog of war. I belonged here. I knew the game. Now I needed to rise to the level of play that I knew I was capable of. No one was going to hand that to me. I just needed to do it. We walloped Washington State 28–3 in our next game, and my level of play rose a bit, but still I wasn't satisfied.

We lost to Oregon after that. Beat Stanford. Then lost to California, then lost again to Oregon State. I think all the players on the team were feeling frustrated by then—and frustration has a way of bubbling to a boil if you let it. Kahlil Bell came back from his injury. He was a senior, an enforcer. He was one of those guys who if a younger guy messes up, he'll hold him accountable for it and get him. In one of our practices sometime around then, he fumbled. This time the tables were turned, and I told him to shape up.

Now, I know this today—I should have kept my mouth shut. A guy like Kahlil is already going to be hard on himself, so he doesn't want anybody else telling him that. But I wasn't thinking that back then. I was just thinking, *Hey, he calls other guys out when they fumble, so I'm going to call him out when he fumbles.* And that didn't go over so well, as you can only imagine. Today I can see why Kahlil undoubtedly thought, *Who's this young buck telling me what to do?! I've been here five years*—he had a medical redshirt one year—*and he's not even played a full season yet.* Kahlil just glared at me and we went on to the next drill. Then something snapped, because he came over to me, pushed me, and said, "Don't you ever disrespect me again!"

I pushed him back and said, "Hey—you gonna yell at us? It's a two-way street!"

We pushed each other a couple of times. There were no punches thrown. That was the end of it. But, wow, the way the media grabbed hold of that and blew it up to make it something it never was, man, you would have thought it was World War III.

We're okay today, Kahlil and me. I know now that I should have shown Kahlil more respect. We joke about it these days. In any football practice, guys are aggressive and competitive, and you're gonna have scuffles. Football's an aggressive sport. The media was just looking for something to write about.

So, I was gaining confidence, but that first season still proved hard going for me. I had some strong runs and some good play, but it wasn't good enough.

While playing Arizona State in November, we were on the 21-yard line in the second quarter when our quarterback, Kevin Craft, got sacked hard and fumbled the ball. I scrambled and recovered the fumble, then stood with the ball in my right hand, mistakenly thinking the play was dead. One of the Arizona players swatted the ball out of my hand and another Arizona player picked it up and sprinted for the end zone. He scored a touchdown, and Arizona led 7–3. We ended up losing 34–9, and we lost our next and final game against USC, 28–7. That meant our season was finished, and I couldn't help thinking what might have happened if I'd joined up with USC instead of UCLA. But I quickly put that thought out of my mind. UCLA was a great school with a strong football program. We had nowhere to go but up.

It wasn't all bad that year. Not at all. Around midseason, I got the chance to encourage a young hearing-impaired quarterback named Ramon Johnson, who played Pop Warner and wouldn't wear his hearing aids. His mother had read a couple of articles about me and asked if I could help. I said sure, so Ramon and his mom came to practice.

At that practice, I did whatever I normally do, which means I sometimes need to adjust my hearing aids, particularly after a hit. I guess seeing me adjust my hearing aids like that made a good impression on Ramon, because he and I talked after the game.

"We both have hearing problems," I said, "but everybody else has problems, too. For us to go out there and play, we need to overcome a lot. But we're blessed because we can still do this. Our hearing problems don't affect our play. We can still play the game."

He was smiling when he left, and I heard he was wearing his hearing aids at his next practice. That felt good to hear. I'd talked to kids on and off before, and people sometimes called me a role model, but I need to be clear that I don't think of myself that way—not then and not today. I love talking to kids and seeing the lightbulb come on for them. I feed off that energy. If a kid wants to talk, then whenever possible I'll take the time to stop and listen. But I'm just a dude who goes out there and deals with what I need to. I started out wanting to play one game in the NFL and did whatever I could do to make that happen. It's just me trying to live my life, plain and simple. I'm not trying to become someone who kids look up to. I'm not trying to become somebody famous. I'm definitely not trying to become a celebrity. I'm just living my life. If telling my story to others helps them find the confidence to accomplish their dreams, then I'll tell my story. But I'm just trying to be Derrick Coleman Jr. and to live the best life I can.

All in all, my freshman year ended up being okay. As a team, we had a lot of injuries and played a lot of freshmen. We ended up going 4-8 for the year, which meant the whole team was developing, not just me.

On a positive front, I saw action in ten games, including one start against Washington where I ran for 42 yards on 10 carries. Overall, I was second on the team in rushing yards with 284 for the season. That meant I averaged 5.4 yards per carry. "Five yards at a time" became a good motto to live by.

I had several really good games. When we played Fresno State, I led the team with 86 yards rushing, including a 44-yard run down the field. That felt like I was being my old self again. No touchdowns my freshman year, but I was just getting going.

———

My sophomore year also went okay. I started understanding my role more on offense. In many ways, I was still a young buck trying to learn. Coach Neuheisel came up with this motto for the year: "Run the ball or die trying." I liked that and gave it all I had.

In our game against San Diego State, I had one excellent 29-yard scoring run. It was my first carry of the game, and I was thinking, *Man, this is just like high school again. I'm back.* But in the next game, against Tennessee, I couldn't duplicate any of that old magic. Mama always told me to stay focused, stay humble, and stay hungry. I was learning that lesson, that was for sure, bit by bit by bit.

All the running backs were still on the team, still in the race to be starter. Nobody ended up redshirting, so it was still seeing who the best man out there was. We had a lot of bodies in the running back position, and the coach would play whoever was doing well at the time. Sometimes that was me. Most of the time it was somebody else.

We ended up going 7-6 for the season, better than my freshman year, but still not quite good enough. On the positive side, I appeared in all thirteen games and made one start at Washington State. Again, I was second on the team with 244 yards rushing.

In spite of all the time I put in on the football field, I still found time to help out off the field whenever I could. Saticoy Elementary School in North Hollywood has a program for hearing-impaired students, and they invited me to come and talk. My big message to them was that nobody should be embarrassed about wearing hearing aids. Each person in life has difficulties he or she needs to overcome. Fortunately, hearing problems can be helped. The key is to overcome fears and achieve goals.

That was a good time, but overall I'd say I never quite found my rhythm that year in the game. There were still more obstacles I needed to overcome.

———————

Near the start of my junior year at UCLA, I came to the conclusion that I was not going to be the star player I'd been in high school. I don't know why it took me this long to figure out.

The competition in high school can be intense, but even then it's not the same sort of fierce competition that you find in college. In high school, if you have skills and drive and work ethic and if you're fast and strong, you're pretty much guaranteed to be a standout player.

In college, every player has skills and drive and work ethic and is fast and strong. College pretty much only takes the high school standouts. So it's harder to have execution on a football field in college when you're competing with a team full of former high school stars. By *execution* I mean it's harder to push past players from the other team and dominate, because the other team's full of former high school standout players, too. When you're up against that kind of competition, and you're playing shoulder to shoulder alongside that kind of competition, it's harder to gain yardage and ultimately score. That's execution.

I was okay with this realization, and I knew I needed to help out the team and make my mark wherever I could. I started getting involved in special teams more, excelling in punt and kickoff returns, and I made my mark there. But what I still really wanted to do was win the starting position as a running back.

Kahlil Bell had graduated by then. Johnathan Franklin had started most of the year before. He'd had some fumbling problems at the start of the current year, but he had a better training camp than me, which meant the gate was still wide open. I dug deep and gave it all I had. The coaches decided I was going to be the starter—and initially I was. Our first game was against Kansas State. I did all right, and Johnathan did well, too, even though we lost the game 31–22.

Then we played Stanford.

Stanford had a fierce squad that year, and the game proved a tough battle from moment one. We were playing at the Rose Bowl, and a lot of my family and friends were in the stands. Both my mom and dad were there, as well as a lot of friends from high school days. Even my big brother, Keyon, was there. He'd had a rough go of it for a season, gotten into some trouble, and had even spent a while in jail. But he was doing better, aiming for solid ground, cheering me on. Everyone was sitting on pins and needles, cheering with all their might, hoping we'd be victorious.

It was the third quarter, and we were driving hard. I mean, really hard. Stanford was pushing back at us with everything they had. Every hit was bone-crunching. Nobody was holding back anything. Our teams felt evenly matched in skills, passion, and aggression, but they were killing us in what matters most—points. They scored touchdown after touchdown, while we couldn't even get on the board.

About halfway through that quarter I got the ball after the snap and charged down the sideline. I could see an opening in the distance. If I could just push a little harder, then we might finally see some daylight in this game. I shook off a player, but another one grabbed on. Two guys made a grab at me and slowed my stride. Then guys torpedoed themselves into me. All forward motion stopped. I went down hard and felt a crush of guys thud on top of me. The ball rolled loose. It all happened so quick. It was mayhem. Everybody scrambled. Everybody dove. Whistles screamed. The fans were going nuts. Then the ball was dead. Definitely dead. Then I felt one more huge thud as one last final player came in and hit the pile—hard.

I should explain that one of the biggest fears every football player has is that he'll get hit so hard he'll never recover. Think about it this way: the injury rate for professional football players is something close to 100 percent. I mean—*every* player gets hurt. The rate for college players isn't much less than that, but it's no secret to any player that getting hurt is a given in this game. For instance, after Johnathan Franklin finished at UCLA, he was picked up by the Packers and had a great season until he suffered a serious neck injury in a game against the Vikings. Fortunately, Johnathan healed up. But it proved a career-ending injury for him. His career in the NFL ended after a total of only eleven games. That's how brutal football can be.

So there I was in the Stanford game under a pile of defensive players. One by one, they peeled off me. I'd been hit in the back of the head and was still on the ground.

All was dark.

And I wasn't getting up.

9

GRADUATION DAY

My mama watched all of this unfold from the stands. Almost instantly, she put two and two together. Her boy was lying on the field, knocked out cold from a head injury. The moment it became clear that I wasn't getting up, Mama shot out of her seat at the top of the stairs and made a run through the corridors of the stadium, heading toward where I was lying.

Security is heavy at any college game. Fans just can't run out on the field. I was only out for a few seconds, and I remember that when I came to, I saw medical personnel bending over me. I saw the faces of training staff. Players. Everybody's brow was furrowed, and I could tell something was gravely wrong.

Then I saw Mama, and I wondered, *How did she ever get on the field?*

Then I saw my dad's face, too—he was only a few paces behind her—and I tried to piece it all together to make sense of what just went down.

My body felt limp, like nothing was connected anymore. They did all these tests on me, then strapped me to a backboard, carted me off the field, and put me in an ambulance. We rushed to the hospital.

I didn't know this until later, but all my friends and family immediately left their seats, too. They connected to my mom by phone and texts and figured out what hospital I'd been sent to, then drove over and filled the waiting room.

We spent the next five hours at Huntington Memorial Hospital in Pasadena. Basically, the doctors just took me through their concussion protocol. The issue of my hearing impairment never came up. They looked at X-rays, did various tests, and worked to figure out the extent of my injuries. They just wanted to make sure I was okay and not paralyzed. Can I move my legs, my arms—that was the concern. I felt fine pretty quickly. When they determined all was okay, they put a neck brace on me, told me to slow down, and released me from the hospital. I stood up, walked down the hallway and out through the security doors, and went out into the waiting room.

Man, the feeling is hard to describe when you see a pile of people waiting for you in a room like that. My friends just mobbed me. I knew I was loved. They'd been worried and praying. A few of them had been crying, thinking that I'd been seriously hurt. I felt so grateful. Seeing all those friends was a reminder to me that I'd come a long way since my grade school days, when I was getting teased every day on the playground. I thanked them all for being there and filled them in. It was only a concussion, nothing worse. Everything was going to be okay. We were all laughing and felt relieved.

The next game was against Houston, and I sat that out. They had a guy who was throwing off the charts, but we beat them anyway, 31–13.

After that, the coaches started to work me back in little by little. The next game was against Texas, and in the meantime, thanks to my concussion, they'd put Johnathan Franklin back in the starter role. He was doing well, so I didn't get my job back, and word was they were going to start him the rest of the season. I'd still be a backup and play on special teams, where I knew I excelled, but I felt a bit discouraged. I decided to do my best anyway. A lack of starting position wasn't going to hold me back.

Jonathan and I ended up both playing in the Texas game. We both did well and had a lot of long runs. We beat the Longhorns 43–12, and that was the game that really put me on the map with scouts, according to my agents. The Chicago Bears expressed interest in me after that. I rushed for 94 yards on 16 attempts, had a 29-yard touchdown run late in the game, and I was feeling good. My head was healed. My confidence was up.

We played Washington State after that, and both Johnathan and I ran all over the Cougars, weaving our ways up the field time and time again. I had 180 yards. Johnathan had 210. We beat the Cougars 42–28, and the press and fans started to compare Johnathan and me to thunder and lightning. Johnathan would start a game with a bang and wear down the other team. Then I'd come in, execute plays at the speed of light, and take us home. Elsewhere in the press, they started to call us "Franklin and Bash," like a boxer with a one-two punch. I didn't like that nickname as much, but it reflected the aggression against the opponent that I could easily adopt in any game.

I ended up playing in eleven games my junior year, despite having only the two starts at the beginning of the season. My per-game rushing average of 44.27 yards ranked me thirteenth in the Pac-10. I averaged 5.9 yards per carry and was second on the team with 5 touchdowns. On special teams, I made 10 tackles and won UCLA's Tommy Prothro Award for Outstanding Special Teams Player. I had one brilliant 72-yard run against Washington State, the longest of my college career. All in all, a great year. We set the mark.

That year, my junior year at UCLA, turned out to be one of my most favorite. It had started out rocky, but in the end we found the buyer. We found what worked. I was playing with a stronger work ethic, understanding what I needed to do more to make a difference on the team. I'd seen how nothing is given to you; you need to work hard for everything you get. My response to that was that even if I wasn't a starter, I was never going to relent.

My senior and final year at UCLA started out much the same way, with everybody playing hard, and me again not in the starter position.

Johnathan had redshirted earlier, so he had the option of playing both his senior year and one more of college ball after that if he wanted. We weren't rivals, I'd say, even though we were both gunning for the same job. We became pretty good friends, actually. We developed a camaraderie born out of mutual respect. Johnathan would run his heart out every game, and that only succeeded in elevating my level of play.

Before the start of each game, Johnathan and I had this saying. Whoever saw the other one first would say, "Go get your money!" And the other guy would grin and nod. Johnathan began the year with a fumbling problem, so I was like, "Sorry, but I'm going in." Then he improved and went back in as a starter. I was able to put my ego on the sidelines, waiting and working, believing that the skills that both Johnathan and I brought to the team only made us collectively stronger.

That year, without being a starter, I was able to fine-tune a constant "be ready" philosophy. Any time I took the field, I was a hard charger, and one newspaper article called me a "mallet-in-waiting." If this had been high school football, I would have sought only the limelight, but I guess I'd matured bit by the time I was a college senior. More than the limelight, I wanted daylight—that promise of moving the ball down the field for the end zone.

We lost our opener to Houston, then won our second game against San Jose State. Then we lost against the Texas Longhorns, then won against Oregon State. The rest of the season pretty much progressed like that, a win and a loss, a win and a loss.

Despite the ups and downs, it felt like a strong season all in all. A lot of things clicked. I got along well with all the coaching staff and players. I got to where I could read Head Coach Rick Neuheisel's lips from thirty-five yards away. He'd be on the sidelines, and I'd be in the middle of the field, and we could understand each other perfectly.

The game of football itself had become more intuitive to me. I wasn't out there thinking about playing in the NFL so much as I was just going hard and smart in every game we played. Part of that was because I was feeling more comfortable and confident at that level of play than ever before. Part of it was that I worked my butt off. I got to where I'd watch game film over and over again, studying our opponents, sometimes studying the same film as much as two dozen times before a game. I knew that if I did go on to play in the NFL, I would need to work twice as hard as I'd ever worked before.

In our game against Arizona State I rushed for 119 yards and had two touchdowns, one of those coming on our final drive, during the last minute of play. We won the game by a hair's breadth, 29–28, and the crowd went absolutely nuts.

By the end of the season, I'd appeared in all fourteen games and played as both a running back and on special teams. I won the Tommy Prothro Award again for Outstanding Special Teams Player, as well as the Paul I. Wellman Memorial Award for All-Around Excellence. I led the team with 11 touchdowns and was ranked second on the team with a career-best 765 rushing yards (that's a lot of yards), and I had several 100-yard games. Overall, I was one of only five Bruins named to the 2011 Pac-12 All-Conference team, and I earned second-team honors as a strong performer on special teams. I got a lot of press and signed autographs at the end of every game.

All that, without being a starter.

College was more than football to me, although football was definitely a huge part of it. The older I got, the more I understood just how the world is, how it operates. I liked the person I'd been in high school, and I didn't want to ever change who I was at the core. I was a hardworking individual, and I only wanted to further that, never swerve from that.

Choosing the right major took a while. I liked math, but didn't want to become an engineer. I liked science, but didn't want to be a doctor. Eventually, I chose political science and took a lot of courses about public policy, American politics, and international relations. I liked the thought processes involved in that course of study. You needed a mind like a lawyer to do well in poli sci, always thinking one step ahead. Johnathan Franklin majored in the same thing, so it was good to talk shop with him about our schoolwork, not just football. My cumulative GPA toward the end of college hovered right around 3.1, and I was named to the dean's list more than once, even during football season.

I dated a girl named Erica for almost two years. She stayed on campus, but her family lived nearby, only about ten minutes in L.A. traffic, so we'd go over there a lot. Eventually we broke up, but we remained friends. Right before my senior year, my good friend Dani introduced me to a girl named Keilani, who played softball for the University of California, Santa Barbara. It took a while, because Keilani didn't want to give in at first, but we started dating and ended up dating the first year after I graduated, too.

With my spiritual life, I got involved with an interdenominational sports ministry called National Fellowship of Christian Athletes. We had a Bible study once a week, and I went to church a lot of Sundays, usually with my mom.

In UCLA's quarter system, graduation day was set for June 13, 2012. There was no way I was going to miss it. That spring, I had a lot on my plate, with teams flying me here and there, and I was definitely thinking about football a lot. But I was also thinking about my schoolwork. Nobody else in my family had ever gotten a degree like the one I was aiming toward—a bachelor's from UCLA, one of the best schools in the nation. And in this world, you gotta have a college degree to get a good job. It felt momentous for my whole family. I wanted that slip of paper for myself. I wanted it for my parents. I wanted it for all my younger cousins so they'd know the bar was being set high.

One of the best things that kept me going was remembering something from one of the player development reps on the team. He'd brought everybody in early in the season and said, "Commitment is not a switch that you can just turn on or off anytime you want. Your 'work hard' switch needs to be constantly turned on. When you're out on the practice field, you're committed to the game, and you want to bring that same level of dedication to the classroom, too. If you have a lazy mindset in your schoolwork, then you'll have a lazy mindset on the field. Whatever you do, make sure to work hard at it."

On June 13, 2010, I flew back to Los Angeles from the East Coast and walked across the UCLA graduation stage. All my family was there, cheering and applauding. It felt good to know that I'd played a sport and gotten a degree all at the same time. I'd worked hard at football, and I'd worked hard at my schoolwork, too. *Derrick Coleman Jr., college graduate.* I liked the sound of that a lot.

But I'm getting a little ahead of myself.

Remember back at the start of the book, when I told you that my big goal was just to play in one regular-season NFL game? It's a fact that I didn't get drafted into the NFL back in February during my senior year when the draft took place, and since I didn't get drafted, for a little bit of time I thought my dream was crushed.

But, just like that preacher told us all one day in church, sometimes when you're at the back of the line things have a way of very quickly turning around so you find yourself at the front.

No, I didn't make the draft. But I soon found out that my dream wasn't dead after all. And where I was right before my graduation ceremony had everything to do with me living out my dream of playing in the NFL.

10

BIG HOPE/BIG DISAPPOINTMENT

So, shift into reverse and back up in time from my graduation to a few months earlier, April 28, 2012. There I was, late Saturday afternoon on the last day of the NFL Draft, shooting hoops with my friends in the driveway of my mom's house in Fullerton, waiting for a phone call that would change my life forever.

An hour passed and another hour passed and another hour passed, and still no phone call. The sun over Los Angeles was starting to head for the horizon, and my phone was dead in my hands, as dead as my dream. I was feeling as low as a piece of roadkill. When it came to the 2012 NFL Draft, I was most certainly not going to be picked.

And that's when another call came.

This one was from one of my agents, Mark Bloom, who talked

to me about going to the NFL as a free agent. We in our family were all new to this, remember, so what we didn't realize yet is that there's another "draft" that takes place after the official draft. The second draft is not actually a draft. It's a negotiation process where teams will pick up extra players as free agents. If you're a free agent, it means you're eligible to play in the NFL and you can sign a contract with any team that offers you one. You might be a veteran player whose contract has expired. Or you might be an undrafted college player, like me.

I tell ya, when we got that call, suddenly the atmosphere at my house went from solemn to excited. I was back in the game. My big dream was back in sight.

What Mark explained to us is that there are pros and cons to being a free agent, particularly if you've never yet been in the NFL. The cons are you don't have the prestige of being drafted, and your signing bonus—if you get one at all—is a lot less. That might sound trivial, to be concerned about a smaller signing bonus, but sometimes in the NFL a signing bonus is the only guaranteed salary you'll ever see. If you get injured on your first day on the field, depending on how your contract is written, a team can sometimes cut you loose right then and there. Or you might sign as a free agent but not make the roster, which also means you're out of a job.

The signing bonus for a first- or second-round draft pick can be big money. I'm talking big, *big* money. For instance, in the 2014, the year this book is being written, the number one NFL Draft pick, Jadeveon Clowney, was paid more than $14.5 million by the Houston Texans as a signing bonus, part of his overall four-year, $22.3 million contract. Few players make that kind of coin. But even if you're a seventh-round pick, the signing bonus can be as much as $100,000. Sometimes even more.

By contrast, the signing bonus for a rookie free agent is around five thousand bucks. Sometimes nothing at all. Now, at that point in my life as a college student in 2012, I wasn't saying no to five thousand dollars—know what I mean? That was five thousand bucks I didn't have before, so I'll take it. That was my attitude.

There are two big positives to being a free agent. First, you'll get a good shot to play in the NFL, which is what I really wanted all along. Second, you'll sometimes have a better selection of where you want to go.

That's what Mark Bloom was telling me over the phone. The bad news was that I wasn't going to be drafted. We knew that much. But the great news was that I still had several teams interested in signing me on as a free agent. Eight good, strong teams, in fact— the Lions, Dolphins, Rams, Vikings, Seahawks, and a couple more. I could choose what team I went to. So we narrowed it down, and the two best opportunities were Miami or Minnesota. The offers were good, they were right on the table. This was my big chance.

Mark told me to go talk to my folks about it and call him back as soon as I could. I hung up, and my mom and dad and I all went inside the house so we could talk it over in private. We called my agents back to get more information, then called a couple of scouts for the same reason. And people were calling us back. The phone rang off the hook for quite a while there. Then it was decision time.

The big difference to me was that Miami wanted me to play full-back, while Minnesota wanted me to play running back. I wanted to play running back, because that was the position I knew best.

By that point, I'd only played fullback for one week of my life, for an all-star game. So it made sense to go for a position where I had a greater knowledge of what to do on the field.

Part of the big question in it all was what team would give me the best chance of making the squad. See, if you sign as a free agent, that doesn't mean you're guaranteed to play. It's more like you come and compete for a spot, and often that means competing against three to five other guys who are all trying for the same thing. So what you need to figure out beforehand is which players are already signed for that spot on a particular team, where they might be weak or strong, who the GM and coaches are bringing in new, who they already have waiting in the wings, who's injured and how badly— that kind of stuff. All you can do is make your best educated guess, then go for it.

Minnesota was looking really good to us. For running backs, in 2010 they'd drafted Toby Gerhart, a running back who'd had a great career at Stanford but hadn't played much in Minnesota yet due to injuries. They also had Adrian Peterson, who'd just torn his ACL, a bad injury in football, so he wasn't available for camp. That meant they were looking for an all-around running back for their third position. Vying for the role would be me and three other guys: Jordan Todman, a productive rookie coming from the University of Connecticut; Matt Asiata, an all-conference standout from the University of Utah; and four-year veteran Lex Hilliard, who'd just come from the backup running back slot in Miami.

Okay, I thought, *let the best man win.*

I called Minnesota and told them that I definitely wanted to join their team. We got a contract from the Vikings, signed it, then faxed it back. Then we called back the other teams and told them, politely, that we were regretfully declining their offers. In this business you never want to be a jerk. You'll need opportunities down the road, and you never know what team you might get a shot to play with next if your first choice doesn't work out.

Then I walked outside and told the rest of my family and friends the big news. They were all really happy for me—for *us*. We'd all come a long way, yeah, we had. My good friend Brian was there, and he's a huge Dolphins fan and had a hunch that Miami was looking at me, so I wondered what he might think to learn that I'd just turned down his favorite team. But Brian was all smiles. "You don't want to play for the Dolphins," he said. "You want to play running back, not fullback. You made the right choice."

Me personally, I wasn't celebrating quite yet. I'd just made one of the biggest decisions of my life, and we all felt good that we'd picked the right team. But it takes me a while to process things, and I knew the hardest work was still ahead of me. All I wanted was one opportunity, and I was getting that opportunity right now. If I messed up, then that was going to be on me. But at least I'd get that one shot to prove myself.

I felt pressure from a number of sources. I knew that if I earned a spot with the Vikings, history would be made, although I was trying hard not to think about that much or let that motivate me. In the history of the NFL, only two other players have been deaf. I felt honored at the prospect of joining the ranks of these men.

The first was Bonnie Sloan, a defensive tackle with the St. Louis Cardinals back in 1973. He played only four games, then injured his knee and was released at the end of the season.

Then came Kenny Walker, who'd become deaf as a child due to meningitis. He was a defensive lineman with the Broncos in 1991 and 1992.

Neither of them had played offense, which would be the history-setting part for me if I made it onto the Vikings squad. So I knew this was my time. This was my one big chance to make it as the first deaf player on offense in the NFL.

I'd say that those days right around the draft were the first time the potential to make history ever clicked in for me. We talked about it as a family, and I knew my family was proud of that possibility. Today, ask me if I'm a history maker and I'll tell you that all I've done is help open a door a little wider. I've opened it for the hearing-impaired community, but also for any other people who folks might have written off. I didn't do anything special to make it into the NFL. All I did was work hard. Real hard. And I didn't listen to the people who told me it couldn't be done.

My friend Dani texted me the other day. She's a softball coach at a university, and she told me that she'd just offered a scholarship to a hearing-impaired softball player. Maybe that's partially because of my influence. The hearing-impaired community isn't getting passed up as much anymore. It feels really good to know the door's open a bit wider. That's the kind of history that matters most to me.

I flew out to Minnesota right after signing with them as a free agent so I could attend their three-day minicamp. The team was already busy with Optional Training Activities (OTAs), which means team members were lifting, doing workouts, and going through trainings with helmets but not pads yet. Sort of like spring training for baseball.

Lex Hilliard wasn't there yet, but I met Matt Asiata and Jordan Todman. They were strong, but I honestly wasn't worried too much about the competition. I knew all four of us would be competing for the same job, but I wanted that stiff competition around me. It would push me to play the very best I could.

I was shown my locker. It had my name stenciled on it already, along with the NFL logo, which looked pretty cool. But I knew it was located where the rookies stored their gear, on the inside of the locker area. The locker area in Minnesota sort of looks like a big living room, and the veterans have lockers in a different location on the outside of the training area. I placed that mental picture firmly in my mind. I wanted a locker over there on the outside—where the rookies *weren't*. That was my big question: What do I need to do to get a locker over there? What do I need to do to make this squad?

In football, I always try to go out of my way to be nice to the people who work in three specific areas. I mean, I try to be nice to everybody and treat everybody with respect, but I'm particularly mindful of these three strategic positions in football: the equipment guys, who get you all your gear; the athletic trainers, who help bring you back when you get nicked up; and the strength and conditioning guys, who help turn your body into a weapon. That's what your body is in football: a weapon. I mean, in hockey you've got a stick. In baseball you've got a bat. But in football, you don't have anything except your body. That's your weapon.

On my first day at Minnesota, I started talking to one of the equipment guys. He was a survivor, he'd been around. We talked for a while and I asked him, "What do I need to do to make it on this team?"

He didn't miss a beat. "Just go out there and prove yourself," he said in a gravelly voice.

I nodded, looked at him a moment without saying anything, then said, "I appreciate it." I was sincere about it. My dad taught me to say that—and to mean it—because anyone can say a simple "thank you." But when you say "I appreciate it," that means something more. You're treasuring whatever it is that they just gave you. And that's what I was doing with the equipment guy. He was giving me condensed wisdom, and I was sincerely taking it to heart.

We had a meeting that first night where everybody introduced themselves. We went over some plays. I was still concentrating on getting that locker.

The three-day minicamp went well. Each day was filled with training exercises and practices. Each night was studying from the playbook. At the end, I asked the running back coach how I did.

"You've got what it takes," he said. "Go home, and make sure you stay in shape, because I like the way you work—then come back ready to work hard."

Usually I watch movies on a plane, but on that long flight home to Los Angeles I just sat and tried to think. My head was spinning. My gut was full of information. I kept asking myself that same question and trying to answer it—*What do I need to do to get that locker?* I didn't know the answer to that yet, and I churned about what I couldn't control, not knowing the details. When I was back at school, I tried to concentrate on the rest of my schoolwork, but it wasn't easy. I kept training as fiercely as I could, kept up on my schoolwork, and thought about football—that's all I did then.

I wasn't allowed to take a full playbook home from Minnesota, but while at camp I'd made extensive notes—both mental and hand-drawn—and I studied and memorized all I could about the Vikings when back in California. Each night I would reread each play, then say it out loud, then redraw each play, then say it out loud again, time and time again. I wanted to train my mind the absolute best I could so the fog of war wouldn't set in again. I wanted to be overprepared. Once I took the field again, I would know each play, clap my hands on the break, then instantly know the route to go on—as well as know what every other player was going to do.

I'd talked with Jed Collins earlier, who was signed by the Eagles as an undrafted free agent and was represented by my agency, and I knew the necessity of keeping the intensity level up and of fighting hard for my position. Jed had been cut something like thirteen times by eight different teams, and he'd stressed to me the importance of never giving up. One of the biggest things I needed to do to make it into the league was pay attention to detail, Jed said. Like, if you're supposed to run a five-yard burst and then slant right, make sure you don't run four yards or six yards. Run exactly five yards. Be precise. Don't cut anything short. Don't cut anything long. During those last few months and weeks of college, my mind was filled with counsel like that.

James "the Dream" Washington was a UCLA alumnus who'd gone on to play for the Rams, Cowboys, and Redskins. After his NFL career, he'd come back to UCLA as the director of scholarships in UCLA athletics. I'd talked to him a few times on campus and he talked to me again then. "You're going to get your opportunity," he said. "You belong on there." I remember his words specifically, because I noticed he didn't say my position was secure. He didn't say I was guaranteed to *play*. He said only that I was going to get my *opportunity*. He knew how hard it is to make it onto a team.

When my last final exam was over, I flew back to Minnesota for the start of the official training camp, got off the plane, and drove the rest of the way out to the city of Mankato, where the training facilities are located. They'd had six or seven OTA practices by then, so I'd missed a chunk of them, and I carried with me three huge suitcases on that trip.

Remember that number. *Three*.

It means I took a lot of my stuff with me, and why? Because I was so certain I was moving to Minnesota for good. There was a never-die attitude that accompanied my packing. I was putting everything I had into this opportunity, burning my ships on the shores of America so I couldn't return to the Old World, living like my dream was guaranteed to come true. I knew the type of player I was. All I needed to do was prove it to the team.

Well, I know now that sometimes that can be a good attitude to have. But sometimes that attitude can get you into big trouble, as I was about to learn.

———

You can't have more than ninety players on a team at the start of training camp—that number is dictated by the official NFL rules.

As far as I could tell, all ninety Vikings were present at the start of the official training camp. Out of those ninety, right around half of them—forty-five—were returning players and early-round draft picks who were guaranteed a job.

That left the other forty-five guys, me being one of them, competing for spots. How many spots? I knew the odds. After the fourth preseason game, the roster would be trimmed to 75. After the third preseason game, it would get further sliced to 53 players—and even then, only 46 guys would dress for actual games. The math was simple. All told, 45 hard-driving hungry free agents were fighting for 8 open spots.

On the first day of training camp, I got out on the field twenty minutes before I needed to be there. I wanted to be first on the field, last to leave. Other players started to appear. I recognized quarterback Christian Ponder, wide receiver Jerome Simpson, center John Sullivan, and more. These guys were the real deal, the same guys I saw on TV. I felt a bit starstruck, I must admit.

We did some stretches and drills, then started with a scrimmage. I got a handoff and ran a quick five yards. Any butterflies disappeared with that first play. I realized I was doing the same repetitive motion I'd done since high school. Everything in the NFL was faster, though, and everybody knew what they were doing. I reminded myself to keep fighting as hard as I could.

I can honestly say that being deaf didn't factor into anything for me the whole time I was with the Vikings. At least, I don't think it ever did. After two years of Pop Warner, four years of high school football, and another four years of college ball, I knew how to play football by then and I knew what I needed to do. I think the Vikings coaching staff asked me about it right at first, but it was a really brief conversation, and it never came up with them ever again. I told the quarterback about it, like I always do, just to make sure I could read his lips during a huddle, but it was never a big deal.

The next three practices went well. Each day we were on the field. Each night I was up in my room, picturing and committing to memory play after play.

My graduation from UCLA was set for June 13, my mom's birthday, so I got special permission to fly home for that. Briefly I considered not going. Football was my first priority. But I talked to the coaches about it, and football was everything to them, too, but they knew that college graduation only comes around once, so they were okay with me leaving. I quickly flew home, walked the stage, wished my mother a happy birthday, then quickly flew back.

Over the next two weeks of training camp, I gave it my all. Each day was a tight schedule filled with sweat, pain, and unwavering concentration. I was shocked at how many fans showed up to watch the Vikings practice. I'd seen fans at UCLA practices, but seeing this many people show up unnerved me just a bit.

I'd say I had a good training camp but not a great one. As much as coaches want you to be precise about doing everything they tell you to do, they also want you to simply go out and play. It's a fine balance. You need to follow their orders exactly by the book. Then you also need to be "you" on the field. I had the book down cold. The being "me" part was more difficult. I realized I was playing too self-consciously, always wanting to be flawless. The quest for perfection was rattling me. I know now that it actually slowed me, because I needed to concentrate about the "me" they wanted me to be, rather than just play and be the "me" I actually was.

For the first preseason game, August 10, 2012, we flew to San Francisco. Now, you've got to realize that my parents were great at taking me to a lot of things while I was growing up. They were both busy working full-time jobs and in spite of that did well at giving me every opportunity they could. But you also have to realize that while I had seen hundreds of football games over the years, I'd never actually been to an NFL game before that moment, not even to watch. The first game I went to was the first game I played at.

I didn't know what else to do other than do what I always did. I warmed up, suited up, and put my pads on—going through the pregame rituals like always. Both of my parents came to see that game. When I went out onto the field, I saw their faces up in the stands of Candlestick Park. My dad came down, and I introduced him to Vikings head coach Leslie Frazier.

The coin was tossed, and the game started without a hitch. I noticed immediately that the play was a lot faster than during practice. For the entire first half I stood on the sidelines, and as much as I was itching to be out on the field to prove myself, I was okay at first with just watching. It gave me a chance to take mental notes. The quick, hard, rough-and-tumble play felt a bit like when we'd played Texas back in UCLA. I knew I could do this if given the right chance.

During the second half, I got my opportunity to go out and play. With that first preseason NFL game, I don't remember any carries. I don't remember any yardage gained. It's all a blur to me now. But I do remember I fumbled one pass. *That* I remember well. I don't know why I dropped the ball. I have great hands. We lost the game 17–6, and afterward I remember being very harsh with myself. I knew that if I kept playing the way I was playing, I wasn't going to earn that locker.

We flew back to Minnesota and returned to practicing. I had a couple of good days of practice. I was killing it on special teams, just running hard through the veterans, which they didn't appreciate at the time. I didn't care—I knew they'd love me later for hitting that hard when we were all playing in regular games.

Our second game was a week later against the Buffalo Bills. I got on the field on special teams and I could have made a good tackle, but I was going too fast while racing down the field and didn't slow down enough to find my control. The rest of the game went okay. I wasn't able to get any opportunities to run. I got a screen pass, but nothing much. No yards gained. We won 36–14.

A week later we played the San Diego Chargers. That game went bad for me. Really bad. For a while I was killing it on special teams. The Chargers had a running back named Jackie Battle, a six-foot-two, 240-pound veteran who I used to watch on TV, and I really admired him. I was running down the field and Jackie was running toward me with the ball. This was my big opportunity to tackle a legend. I had him, too. I totally had him—but my mind was wrapped around that fact long before it became a reality. Before I could reach Jackie, my foot got snagged by the turf, and I felt a sharp pain shoot up my leg. I missed Jackie Battle by a mile and cursed myself for that, but what was really on my mind at the moment was my toe. The pain was agonizing.

Immediately I knew what the problem was. They call it "turf toe," where your toe gets hyperextended. I was in pain something fierce, but there was no way I was going to tell anybody. I needed to keep playing to prove I was anything more than deadweight on the field.

Things went from bad to worse. The next time the ball came to me, I fumbled it. When I came off the field, the coach growled, "What are you doing?" Meaning: Fumbles don't happen, so don't do it again!

The next time I went on the field, I got the ball and fumbled it yet again. This time when I came off the field, I tried to ask the coach what happened. He brushed me off with four little words— "Don't worry about it." Inwardly I winced. I remembered what Wayne Moses, my running back coach at UCLA, had told me once: "The day I stop correcting you is the day you need to transfer." That means if a coach isn't correcting you, he's given up on you. The Chargers beat us 12–10, and I knew my time was short.

I didn't sleep the night after the Chargers game. I tossed and turned, my mind wide awake, my body banged up, my spirit feeling low. Maybe I dozed for thirty minutes. If I was going to redeem myself, I needed a miracle.

The next morning I decided to break my secret about my toe. Maybe that would buy me a bit more time. They fixed up my toe, but later that day, when the general manager made his first cuts from 90 to 75, a guy came around and told me to go up and see the GM.

A long, dry swallow went down my throat. I hoped that at the very least they'd keep me around on the practice squad. You're cut from the roster at that point, but at least you're around the franchise, you're drawing a small weekly salary, and there's always the slim chance you could get called up to a backup position on the team. I knew that I hadn't been playing like "me"—not the Derrick Coleman Jr. who knew how to play football. The level of play I'd demonstrated in preseason wasn't the level of play I could produce.

The visit to the general manager's office was brief. Sure, there was a mention of bringing me back for the practice squad, but they first wanted to check out Jordan Thomas, who'd injured his hamstring earlier.

I knew what that meant.

I packed my bags—all three of my huge suitcases—and got on the plane to head home. I wasn't crying or anything like that, but I was hurting real bad inside. I felt like a failure. I knew I'd let down my family and friends. I didn't want to face anybody. I couldn't look them in the eye. I called my mom first, and we talked some. Then I texted my girlfriend, Keilani, to tell her I got released—as much as I liked her, I didn't even want to see her when I got home. My friends would know soon, but it was hard to picture talking with them yet.

For the next few days at home I iced my foot and did all the exercises I could think of to get it back in shape. You can pick up marbles with your feet. That's about all I did during those days. Ice and marbles, ice and marbles.

On August 30, 2012, the Vikings played their fourth and final preseason game, against the Houston Texans. I didn't want to watch the game. I didn't even want to be around football just then. Matt

Asiata was playing strong. He looked like he was going to earn the third running back slot.

My friend Brandon played football for Whittier College, so Keilani and I decided to attend his game the night of the Vikings game to support Brandon and help get my mind off things. Brandon had a good game, and it was good to see my friends again. While watching the game in Whittier, I also kept tabs on the Vikings-Texans game. Minnesota lost 28–24, but I noted how Jordan Todman also played a great game and had a couple of big runs.

The following day was a Saturday. The Vikings called and told me what I already knew—Matt Asiata had earned the third running back spot, and they were going to put Jordan on the practice squad, not me. I said thanks and hung up the phone. That made it official.

I tried to brush off the news, but inside it was killing me. Keilani asked me how I felt, and I answered her truthfully. I was pissed, angry at myself. All I'd ever wanted was one chance. I had gotten that chance and I'd blown it. I'd come so close to achieving my dream, but I hadn't yet played that one official regular season game—and that would have been only the beginning of what I wanted to do. Hey, I was cut before I'd even made the team.

11

HOW I LEARNED TO PACK A SMALLER SUITCASE

For the next two months—September and October 2012—I stayed at home a lot. I hung out with my friends. I worked out at the gym a lot. But mostly I did nothing. The regular football season started, and every day I scanned the injury report. I wasn't hoping the worst for any other guys. But injuries happen, and I wanted to see if another opportunity would present itself. I wanted to stay ready.

It was harder to find the motivation needed to stay in that level of shape when I didn't have a specific goal to aim toward. A lot of days I didn't feel like going to the gym, but my friends would come by and drag my butt out of the house and we'd go lift or do some drills on the field at the school.

On October 18, my twenty-second birthday arrived. My dad came into my room where I was chilling and said, as only fathers can, "Derrick, I know football is your dream. But you gotta start thinking about what else you might want to do."

We had a good talk. He still believed in me, I didn't doubt that. He was just reminding me that nothing was secure in the world of football. A prudent man will have a backup plan, and as hard as it was to think I might never play in the NFL, I was already thinking ahead. I was networking with business guys, calling my agents looking for other possibilities, researching internships. I went by Troy High School and helped out with their football program a bit. In the meantime, I was thinking maybe I would become a personal trainer. I figured with all the weightlifting and conditioning I'd done over the years, I already knew as much as those trainers did, so I started studying to pass the trainer certification test. Maybe I'd open up my own gym someday.

In the meantime, no opportunities came, and life just felt like a lot of nothing. Honestly, those few months were one of the lower points in my life. I needed to get over my disappointment. I needed to get up and get going again. But I was still down about what happened with the Vikings. I knew I'd been too sure of myself. I'd packed too many suitcases, thinking I'd never be sent home. I was too focused on who I thought they wanted me to become, rather than who I already was. I still needed to learn and grow, sure, but I needed to learn and grow while being comfortable being "me." And I had failed at that.

In the last week of November, I was out on the field at Troy High School doing some drills with my buddies when I got a call from one of my agents. The New York Giants had just called him, and one of their running backs had broken his leg. They wanted to bring me in for a tryout. I was ready to go. Then, right before I got ready to leave for New York, we got another call, this one from the Vikings again. Jordan Todman, who'd been on their practice squad, had been picked by another team, which meant there was an open spot on Minnesota's practice squad again. Was I interested?

Wow. I'd just gone from having no possibilities to having two strong possibilities at once. I couldn't do them both. Minnesota already knew me and knew a bit of what I could do. That provided motivation for me to go there again. But Minnesota was only offering me a shot on their practice squad. New York was offering a tryout for an actual slot on the team. I wanted to play in the game, not be on a practice squad, so I picked the Giants. Before I flew to New York, I asked my agent how much luggage I should take. "Be prepared to be there for at least a week," he said.

I packed one large suitcase this time, not three. But it was still a large suitcase. The biggest one I had. You could argue that I was just following my agent's recommendation, but looking back now, it was a marker of more than that. I was still packing a big suitcase because something more still needed to be whittled away from my ego. I was packing a big suitcase because I still thought I was big stuff. You've got to be confident to play this game—I'm not saying that was my problem. My problem was that along with my confidence came a self-assuredness that didn't yet have a true respect for the fragility of securing a position in the NFL. I was still thinking I was entitled to play. And that wasn't the truth.

Six of us were trying out for the spot in New York. I was the only rookie among them. I checked into a hotel, got up early the next morning, and headed over to the facility. Tom Coughlin, the Giants' head coach, was one of the first people I saw. Back in February, the Giants had beaten the Patriots for the Super Bowl, so I felt in awe of this team as a whole.

That first day, I had a good workout with the Giants and ran some routes. I dropped one pass but it was low and I needed to dive on the ground to get a hand on it. They asked me some questions about my hearing disability but didn't grill me too hard about that. They knew that if I could perform at UCLA, I could perform anywhere. Overall, I thought I was doing pretty well. There were only four games left in the regular season by then, but I still wanted to be signed.

Unfortunately, at the end of that first day they chose two other guys from the six. The rest of us were sent packing. *Wow, that was quick.*

How did I feel? Sure, I was disappointed again. I would have been proud to join the Giants, that's for sure. Yet I was relieved my name hadn't been forgotten entirely. Other teams see whose getting flown out to tryouts, so I was happy to still be in the mix.

Still, I couldn't help but glance at the size of my suitcase as I checked it in at the airport. That one bag was huge. I'd packed for a week, but had been in New York less than twenty-four hours.

Back at home, I just tried to get into the same routine—workouts, practicing, trying to think of the future, trying to always stay prepared.

The very next Tuesday morning, I was sleeping in late at my dad's house. The night before I'd been over at my friend Derek's house, and we'd been up late hanging out. Sometimes I sleep with my hearing aids in. But if I don't have them in, which I didn't just then, I'm dead asleep. Suddenly I heard a loud *bang, bang, bang!* on my bedroom window. That woke me up in a hurry. It felt like the whole house was being rattled.

My mom was outside. "Open the door!" she hollered.

I hurried to the front door and let her in. She was dressed in her nursing scrubs and looked like she'd come straight from work.

"What's going on?" I asked, still rubbing the sleep out of my eyes.

"You didn't see on your phone I been calling you?" Mom asked. (When my cell phone rings, it also lights up.) "Check your phone. Mark's been trying to call you for the past hour and a half."

That was my agent. I ran back to my bedroom and got my phone. It was now 9:30 a.m. Mark Bloom had left a string of messages since eight o'clock. The big news was that Seattle wanted to bring me up for a tryout on their practice squad. A flight was already set for later that same day. Did I want this opportunity or not? When Mark couldn't reach me, he'd called my mom, and she'd left work to come find me. My mother is awesome.

Absolutely I wanted this opportunity. This time I vowed not to blow it. I'd messed up with the Vikings. I hadn't gotten very far at all with the Giants. But I promised myself I wouldn't make any of those mistakes again with Seattle. I didn't have a list of mistakes to never make again so much as I did a renewed mindset. This time I didn't care if it was only a tryout for a team's practice squad. I was going to make it into the NFL, and if a practice squad was my route onto a team, then so be it.

This time I packed carefully—a pair of shoes, a pair of warm sweats, a couple of changes of underwear, my wallet, and my phone. That was all. Everything fit into one small backpack. It was a marker of the new me, the me who'd been refined in the fire over the last few months. I'd learned the hard way that nothing in the NFL is a sure thing. I was going to go try out for the Seahawks' practice squad and put my whole heart into it—that much was sure. Yet this time I was going to check my ego at the door. I wasn't entitled to this.

I didn't even tell my friends I was heading up to Washington. There was no reason to get anyone's hopes up. That same afternoon I went over to the high school and got in one last workout and lifted with the guys. I didn't mention a word of where I was going. That same night I hopped on a late flight for Seattle.

The team put me up in a hotel near Renton, where their training facility is located. The next morning I headed over there—it's called the Virginia Mason Athletic Center, and right away they did some X-rays on my toe to see how well it had healed since my turf-toe incident. My toe looked fine, so I signed a contract to be on their practice squad. It was $5,000 a week, and week to week, meaning I could be let go at any time. Believe me, I was happy to sign that contract. It wasn't exactly big NFL money, but it was a heck of a lot better than what I'd been making for the last couple of months: absolutely nothing.

Right away I noticed a particular atmosphere in the Seahawks training facility. The buildings are new, constructed in a Pacific Northwest Craftsman architecture style, and located on scenic land on the northeast shore of Lake Washington. On the outside of the main building is a huge flag bearing a single number—12, representing the twelfth man on the field with us: the Seahawks' huge fan base.

But it was what was happening *inside* the buildings that impressed me most. Everybody I met—and I mean everybody—smiled at me and said hello. The whole environment was professional but relaxed and friendly. The guy who first showed me around took me on a tour of the various rooms. It was early in the morning and I could smell bacon coming from the dining area. "Yeah, we got the best bacon around here," he said. I believed him, and he added, "You know, all you need to do is just go out there and play. You don't need to worry about anything else."

Wow, I liked the sound of that. I liked everything about the place I'd seen so far. I don't know if you've ever seen that movie *Draft Day*, with Kevin Costner and Jennifer Garner. It's a pretty good movie except that Seattle is made to look like the bad guy. That's not how it is in real life. There's a positive and genuine mentality ingrained in the Seahawks staff whereby they treat everybody with warmth and respect. I know now that it's part of an overall mindset that's taught in the Seahawks' culture. Everybody who works for the Seahawks—from the janitors on up to team owner Paul Allen—are considered valued and needed. Everybody. So if everybody's needed and valued, then everybody's respected. I liked that mindset a lot.

I suited up, put my pads on, and got ready to head out onto the practice field. Just before I went out, I dropped to my knees right by my locker and asked God to watch over me. I thanked Him that He'd given me another opportunity to put the cleats on. I asked Him to help me do my best for His glory. Then I said amen.

It was a Wednesday, the first day of the week for many football teams (game day is Sunday, Monday is a review of game day, Tuesday is a day off), and I was twenty minutes early. The equipment guy was already on the field. Running back coach Sherman Smith came along shortly. He'd been at my Pro Day at UCLA, so I talked to him a bit, mostly just to ask him what my role was on the practice squad.

"Just go out there and give us a good look," he said. Then his voice took a fatherly tone and he added, "You know, Derrick, my wife always makes this pound cake. It's delicious. I've watched her bake, and she takes all the ingredients—a cup of flour, a couple eggs, a teaspoon of vanilla, a bit of sugar—and mixes them all together. When that pound cake comes out of the oven, it's perfect. The team is like that pound cake. Each player is like one of the ingredients. I know how it is on the practice squad, how you can feel like you're not doing much. But every player is important. You're important. Everybody is around here. So no matter what your role is around here, you gotta play it well. That's all we'll ever ask you to do."

I appreciated his advice. I appreciated it a lot. Coach Sherman had a way of putting things in perspective.

The rest of the team and the other coaches came out onto the field. I knew head coach Pete Carroll from his days at USC. He recognized me and said with a grin, "Hey, we got a Bruin in the house. Things might be tough today, so watch yourself out there."

Quarterback Russell Wilson took the field. I respected him a lot. I recognized wide receiver Golden Tate, running back Marshawn Lynch, Earl Thomas, Richard Sherman, Kam Chancellor, Michael Bennett, Doug Baldwin—all the Seahawks' top players. Linebacker coach Ken Norton Jr. noticed me and called out a hearty "Fresh meat!" Every defensive player seemed to turn, grunt, and look my direction. *Oh Lord*, I thought, *this is going to be a long practice.*

Then we went to work.

We had pads on, and for the first bit I was on special teams, just killing it, running as fast as I could, hitting the hard way, trying to make a statement. I knew the other players weren't going to appreciate me, since nobody likes to get drilled that hard during a practice, but I wasn't going to let up unless a coach told me to. The Seahawks' defense quickly seemed particularly fed up with me—and the Seahawks' defense is one of the hardest hitting in the league.

Then it was scrimmage time. Matt Flynn, the backup quarterback, was helping out. It was a play to the left, and Matt turned around and tossed the ball me, but he tossed it too far—just far enough so I needed to stretch to get it. Fortunately, I got a solid grip on the ball and tucked it in tight. Quickly I regained my balance and charged up the field. I thought I'd spotted daylight when Kam Chancellor, the team's strong safety, came from out of nowhere and blew me up with a huge hit square in the shoulder pads. My feet and knees flew up in the air. My back hit the ground. The ball came flying out of my hands, and I thought I had tweety birds around my head. Everywhere around me guys screamed and dove for the ball. It was whistled dead. I got up, and—excuse my language—I said, "Shit."

Coach Carroll was near where I was. "Didn't I tell ya?" he said simply.

One of the newer wide receivers brushed near me and said with a friendly grunt, "I had the same thing happen to me three weeks ago. It's just the team's way of saying 'welcome.'"

I kept going hard. On the next play the ball came to me. Two linebackers charged straight at me. I split them and kept going down the field. That felt good.

All the rest of that day, play after play, I kept going hard. I was glad I'd spent all that time in the gym for all those years, from the Pop Warner days on forward. The work ethic was paying off. At the end of the day I was dead tired, but I still had wind, I still had legs. When the practice was over, I went to the sidelines and started running sprints at 80 percent. First to arrive, last to leave. Coach Carroll came over and said, "You did a good job today. Go get your rest."

My hearing impairment was never an issue in Seattle—not from moment one. Coach Carroll already knew me and my story. His attitude is always that he doesn't concern himself with what problems you've dealt with. The issue that matters most is, can you help the team get the job done now—*Can you help the Hawks win?!*

No player ever reacted in any way to my hearing loss that I ever remember. I talked to Russell Wilson early on, just to explain things to the quarterback like I always did. "Just make sure you look at me" was my standard line. He was willing to help as much as he could and said that if he ever forgot, to remind him. It was no big deal.

The next day we practiced with only helmets, no pads, and I kept up the intensity. It felt like the old me—the "me" I knew from high school days. Confident. But it wasn't a confidence that came from cockiness, speed, size, or raw talent anymore. I was much more humble now. It was a confidence that came from respecting the game and the high level of talent, determination, and drive it takes to play in the NFL.

Already it was the first week of December, and there was a chill in the air. I hit a couple of the bigger guys hard, and I could tell that none of them were too happy with that, but I wasn't going to let up. My job on practice squad was to make sure they worked as hard as they could so they could play as hard as possible in a game.

I met Chandler Fenner that day, another guy on the practice squad. He was new to the team, too, having just been released from the Kansas City Chiefs, and we became fast friends. At the end of that week Seattle played a home game. Practice squad members don't suit up with the team, so we went up to the suites and watched the game from there. I remember Chandler and me sitting next to each other and him saying, "Man, we got to get on that field somehow." I agreed.

The following day was a Monday—they call it "Tell the Truth Monday," when the previous game is analyzed for strengths and weaknesses. (The next day, Tuesday, was a day off, and if a practice squad member is through, then he's usually released on a Monday.)

We did a bit of practice that day, and later when I was taking a shower, one of the players asked if I was through yet. He wasn't being mean, just curious.

"They haven't told me anything" was all I said. I quickly finished my shower, toweled off and got dressed, and hiked up to Coach Carroll's office and knocked. That was a scary few minutes walking from the shower room to the coach's office. My heart started to pound, and I was thinking that if another player asked me if I was still here, then maybe he'd heard something I hadn't. Coach told me to come in and nodded for me to take a seat on the couch while he finished up something.

"Can I talk with you a second?" I asked when he looked up.

He nodded.

"I just want to know where I stand."

Coach Carroll paused. "We really like your work ethic," he said. "We want you to come back next week and keep doing what you're doing." He motioned to the door and went back to his work.

That was our entire conversation.

That was enough for me.

You might think I'd feel comfortable coming back for another week, but there was no way I was feeling comfortable yet. I learned later that Seattle has a different philosophy when asking guys to try out. Very seldom will they bring in a guy for only a day and cut him after that. Instead, they want to see what a guy can do for a few days in a row.

The second week was still tough going, mind you. One of Coach Carroll's mottos is "Always be competing." The way the Seahawks practice is fast and physical, and over the next few days there was no letting up, not for a minute. I kept running fast, tackling hard, concentrating on the ball, always trying to do my best.

If you're staying on with the team for any amount of time, then they take you out of the hotel and put you somewhere else. Mo Kelly, the senior director of player development, referred me to a one-bedroom apartment in corporate housing that was furnished and could be rented for a short term. He found another place for me to rent if I wanted it, but the other place would have been a place of my own, longer term, so I said no. I didn't want to get comfortable. I wanted a place I could leave quickly.

My one small suitcase was still all I needed—each day I changed my socks and underwear, but that was it. I still hadn't talked to any of my friends yet from home. Each day I kept getting all these texts asking where I was. I had seventy-two unanswered texts at one point. But I didn't want to jinx anything. I particularly didn't want to get comfortable. I wanted to say humble, give my all, and prove myself. I was prepared to get cut from the team. I was also focusing, not wanting to miss a second of what was happening around me in the moment.

At the start of my third week in Seattle, a couple of players were sick, and somebody else needed to be somewhere, so they put me in for a few reps with the main team. I made a couple of good runs, just keeping it simple, mostly running straight up the field. Then on one play I got the ball, made a stretch to the left, cut hard up the field, and nobody touched me. It was smooth. When I came back to the huddle, everybody said, "Good run." All except Marshawn Lynch, who said, "Man, you got some wobbly legs." (I learned later that that's his way of complimenting you, so you don't get a big head.)

I had some good other plays, too. I made a couple of high catches, raking the ball in with just my fingertips. Coach gave me a grin and asked, "You got tar on your hands?"

That's about all I did. After that I went back to playing on practice squad. Week after week I kept playing, just working hard at everything I did.

When it came time for the playoffs in January, Seattle beat the Redskins for the wild card, but lost to the Falcons for the division. The Seahawks' season was finished. All in all, I'd played six weeks by then. I wasn't sure what would happen now that the season was over, but the very same day we lost to Atlanta, Coach called me over and said, "We want to pull you back next year." That same day, I signed a three-year deal with Seattle worth $1.5 million. Not all of that was guaranteed money—if I got cut or injured, I'd get a fraction of that. But it meant I was no longer week-to-week. I was officially on the team. I hadn't played yet in a regular game, but I was on my way.

When I was growing up, my dad had always told me that there are two traits that every employer looks for in a potential employee. First, are you a hard worker? And second, are you likable? If a person's lazy or can't even do a job in the first place, he's not going to stay around long. If nobody wants to work with him, why hire a guy like that? The Seahawks' defense acted like they didn't like me because I'd been hitting them too hard, but deep down I knew they appreciated that—and so did the coaches. If you want to rise in your job, then that means working hard all the time. If you're always working hard, sooner or later one of your bosses will see that dedication. It'll pay off.

After the playoffs were finished, the players got a bit of time off. I flew back to California. I still had my one backpack. It's freezing in Seattle in the winter, always raining, always cold, so I'd gone out to the mall near the end of December when I had one of my first paychecks and bought a sweater and some warmer clothes. But I was still traveling light. Always on my toes. Never growing comfortable. Never taking for granted that I was entitled to anything.

I knew that anything could happen when we came back and started OTAs in preparation for the next year's regular season.

For now, traveling light was the way I wanted to keep it.

12

ICING MY ANKLE WITH EVERYTHING I GOT

When the time came for OTAs, I headed back to Seattle. My dad and I loaded up my truck this time and we drove up together. It takes about eighteen to twenty hours to drive from Los Angeles to Renton. I wanted to have a vehicle up there with me this time, along with a few more belongings. Not many, though. I was still rooming in the corporate housing, still not wanting to put down roots. We put an extra twin bed in there, and I shared it with another player. I wanted to save all the money I could. Dad took a flight back to California.

One of the running backs from last season had left the team, which meant Marshawn Lynch and Robert "Turbo" Turbin were still playing that position and the number-three spot was now open. I wanted that job bad. The team had also drafted running backs Spencer Ware and Christine Michael, so it was anybody's game. But God had other plans for me than playing running back.

At the beginning of OTAs, running back coach Sherman Smith told me he wanted me to learn the fullback spot. Fullbacks are getting rarer and rarer in the NFL, but if a good coach knows how to use them right, a skillful fullback can do a lot of good for a team. Michael Robinson was the Seahawks' starting fullback, so if I earned the spot, I'd be his backup. I told Coach Smith that if I had my choice of playing anything, I still wanted to play running back. But if he wanted to try me out at fullback, then I was definitely up for that. I just wanted to play the game.

OTAs went well. The coaches had me train in both positions— fullback and running back. I knew I needed to keep driving hard. When OTAs were over, I drove my truck down to California, left it there, and flew back up to Seattle on my own. I figured if I kept a truck in Seattle, it would prove a distraction to me, and I didn't want anything around me that could cause me to become comfortable. I wanted to stay constantly alert, vigilant, heightened to play the best I could at all times.

Training camp arrived, and all my jitters went out the window. I still knew I could get cut. I'd been there before, but something felt different this time. More permanent. My attitude had changed as much as anything. I knew that this might well be my last shot at making it in the NFL, so I purposely told myself to stop worrying and enjoy the experience while I could. That's right—*enjoy it*. Even when the training hurt. I mean, how many guys can say they've competed for a spot on an NFL team, much less made it onto a team? I knew I was privileged even to have made it so far. This time I wanted to go out and just go play the game. I wanted to be the "me" I knew I could be. I was going to go out there and go hard, give it all I had, and relish every moment I had in this season of life.

The first couple of practices went rough. Whenever I lined up at fullback, I kept getting knocked back from left to right. In this new position I had no technique. Coach Smith kept teaching me, but the learning curve was steep. I texted two friends from home, Brian and Derek, and told them that I was not doing that well. I was getting better each day, and the team knew I'd never played that position before. But in my opinion I wasn't getting better fast enough. Certainly not fast enough to beat out Michael Robinson for the starting position. Maybe not even good enough to become his number two.

One day we were out on the practice field and I was struggling. You look at different guys, and different guys approach the game different ways. Like Marshawn—he's got speed, and he's also real agile on his feet. He can shift at a moment's notice and go any way imaginable. Me, I've always been basically about one thing: beef. I play like a bulldog. I get the ball and charge as hard as I can. If a player on the other team has the ball, then I run him over. Coach Smith was watching me that day when I was struggling, and he called me over and gave me this analogy: "Say you're in a snowstorm and you need to move some snow. What would you do? You'd get your truck and plow it out of the way. That's what you want to do as a fullback. From here on out, think of yourself as a snowplow." He grinned.

That made sense to me. I could learn to play this position only if I could make it my thing. But would I ever be good enough to actually play in a game?

———

The first preseason game was set for August 8 against the Chargers. We flew down, landed, and headed over to Qualcomm Stadium. They were one of my favorite teams, and I looked forward to seeing them up close.

When the game started, I went out there on special teams and got a tackle right on kickoff. Play after play, I kept having a good game. On punt returns I was strong. Eventually I saw some time as a fullback during that game—and then the unthinkable happened.

We had the ball and were close to San Diego's end zone. I got the ball on a flat route and gained a couple of yards, but we were still short. On the next play I got the ball again on another flat route, this one on the other side, and I scrambled all the way into the end zone for a touchdown.

A touchdown!

It was only a preseason game, but I was so pumped up I could hardly stay cool. Honestly, I felt like I did back in Troy High School, like I belonged here. I knew I might never again get that kind of chance, so I tried to take in my surroundings as much as possible, savoring the moment. How did I react when I scored my touchdown? I didn't jump up and down or spike the ball or anything. I got back up and I walked to the huddle, that's what. The other players gave me high fives, but that was it. I'd been in the end zone before in my college days, and I knew that the game wasn't over yet. Once the next play starts, the last play doesn't matter anymore, and there was more work to be done. I'm happy to say we won that game, 31–10.

I knew I still had a long way to go. If I had to grade myself on that first game, I'd give myself an A-plus on special teams, but maybe a C overall on fullback. I'd messed up one block. I was still learning the position. UCLA head coach Rick Neuheisel used to say the definition of good luck is when opportunity and preparation collide. When you're aiming hard for a goal, you keep preparing, always preparing, waiting for your opportunity. When it finally arrives, then you're prepared. That's how I felt during that first preseason game.

The next week, August 17, we played our second preseason game against the Broncos. Man, we whipped their butts, 40–10. I played fullback and did better with my technique. Mentally, I felt wide awake, completely on point. On special teams, I had one good tackle. Overall, it was a solid game for me, nothing crazy.

Right after that game, I flew back to Fullerton. My good friend Brian was marrying his girlfriend, Caitlin. I was a groomsman. They're such great friends to me, they'd even waited for the Seahawks schedule to be released so they could know if I could be in their wedding. The ceremony and reception were perfect. It was great to go home and be among old friends—and it made me a little wistful. For the first time in a long while, I was starting to think I might actually stay in Seattle for a while. I wasn't going to get to see my friends from California again for a good long time.

I felt good, but I also felt a bit uneasy. All that flight back to Seattle I was praying, hoping, thinking how badly I didn't want to mess up my chances with the team. They want a player who gets the job done—period. There aren't any excuses in the NFL.

———

Here's the crazy thing. Remember earlier, how Coach Rick said the definition of good luck is when opportunity and preparation collide?

All that August, Michael Robinson, the starting fullback, was just a little bit off his game. Turned out he wasn't feeling well, losing weight, not playing to full capacity—and I don't consider that good luck for anyone. Eventually he lost thirty pounds, a ton of weight for a man who makes his living as a battering ram. Poor guy. I mean that sincerely, too. Football is that strange mix of competition and compassion, like I talked about earlier. You're eyeing a guy's job because that's how the game is set up, but you genuinely feel for him, too. It turned out that the use of a prescription medication had caused big problems, nearly shutting down his kidneys and liver. He couldn't hold anything down, and his eyes were yellow. After the Denver game it all came to a head. On August 23, we traveled to Wisconsin to play the Packers. Michael stayed home, and—here's where opportunity and preparation collided—I was slotted to start the game.

Right before the kickoff, Coach came up to me and said four short words, "This. Is. Your. Opportunity." I knew exactly what he meant. This was it. This was what I'd been training for my whole life.

So I started as a fullback. That felt good, really good, but I wasn't focusing on celebrating being a starter in the game. I'm sure I called my parents to let them know I was slotted to start, and they were happy about that, but it was still preseason and we knew anything can still happen. It was one opportunity to go out and prove it to them that I could start. That's what it was.

I had a decent game. Not a lot of opportunities came my way, but I held my own. On special teams, I killed it, doing my assignment every time. Two of my former teammates from UCLA played for the Packers now and it was great to see them again. Johnathan Franklin was one of them. Right before the game he said, "You ready to go get your money?"—the same thing we always said to each other at UCLA. We beat the Packers, 17–10.

The fourth and final preseason game was against the Oakland Raiders. Again I started. On the first drive we got down to the goal line. I blocked a dude on the outside, put my bicep on him, and pushed him over like a snowplow. That cleared the way. Turbo Turbin ran right behind me straight into the end zone for a touchdown. That's what a fullback does—clears the way. I was finally doing my job.

Any enthusiasm I might have felt was short-lived, though. On one of the next catches I rolled my ankle. I acted like it was no big deal, and when I came off the field told the trainer to tape it— I needed to keep playing. And I did. We beat the Raiders 22–6, but after the game my ankle was swollen like a softball.

The next day, August 30, was elimination day, where the roster is trimmed from 75 to 53 players. I woke up nervous. I'd had mostly some good games, but I was still traveling light, not sure if I would stay or go. I should have gone straight into the training room to get my ankle worked on some more, but I told myself I wouldn't do that—I didn't want to give the team the smallest speck of a reason to cut me. Instead I took two trash cans and limped to the ice machine two doors down, dragged the ice back to my room, filled the bathtub, and stuck my foot in.

One of my friends texted me early and said he heard a rumor that the Seahawks had released Michael Robinson. I called my agent and asked him if it was true. He said he'd heard the same thing, but that didn't mean I was guaranteed a position—anything could still happen, and even if the Seahawks had released Robinson, they might call up someone else. A lot of other texts came to me early that morning, but I didn't open any of them. I didn't want to look.

Too many options ran through my mind. Chandler had torn his ACL back in OTAs and was on the injured reserve (IR) list already. He and I decided to go out for breakfast. I didn't even want to think about football just then, but that's hard to do anywhere in Renton, where every car you see has a "12" flag flying on its antenna or a Seahawks sticker on its back window. We went to this little hole-in-the-wall joint. I kept my phone near me, praying it wouldn't ring. On draft day, you're waiting with all your might for a call that says, "Congratulations, you made the team." On release day, you're hoping like mad for the exact opposite—that you won't get a call at all.

Right when I cleared away the last of my eggs and bacon, my phone rang. It was my other agent, Derrick Fox. But his voice was bright. "Congratulations," he said. "It's official. They're keeping you around. You made the team."

Wow, I felt excited but apprehensive, too. My agent confirmed that Michael Robinson had been released—and I felt for the guy, I truly did. His release also made me question why the Seahawks were keeping me around. Was it truly because I could get the job done? Or was it only because Michael Robinson had been let go?

All that day mixed feelings went through me. Over and over in my mind I replayed the preseason. Every practice. Every game. I went back to my room and kept icing my ankle, twenty minutes in the ice, forty minutes out. It was still hurting, but the swelling was coming down. I still didn't want to give the team any reason to cut me. I figured they might say something like, "You've been hurt since the game and you didn't tell anyone? You're gone!" Hey— I didn't know.

That night I decided I wouldn't second-guess myself any longer. I concluded that it doesn't matter how you reach your goal, as long as you get there (and don't do anything illegal in the process). It's not where you started from; it's where you finish. Every one of the fifty-three players on every NFL team has got a different story about how he made it onto his team. The stories didn't matter now. We were all there with the same goal: to win, and win big for the team. From here on out, that was what mattered most.

I glanced over at my one small suitcase, sitting near my bed. Slowly I got up from where I was sitting and put that suitcase away in the closet. I wouldn't be needing it today. My story was that

I had just made history by becoming the first legally deaf offensive player in the NFL. The regular season was about to begin, and now my focus needed to shift to that. I would give what came next everything I had.

I limped back to the bathroom and stuck my foot deep into ice.

13

THE SUPER SEASON

When Monday came around, I showed up early at the facility. The swelling on my ankle had gone down a lot, but it was still bothering me a bit, so I had the trainers work on it some. I knew my ankle—and my position with the team—was going to be okay by then, and my anxiety level about my ankle had decreased along with the swelling.

Coach Carroll called a team meeting after that and set it straight for us. I looked around the room at the players. This was the first time I'd seen a trimmed roster of fifty-three players up close, and one of my first thought was, *Whoa, where'd everybody go?* But everyone's hopes were running high, too. There was electricity in the room, a sense of unlimited potential.

"This is it," Coach Carroll said, or something really close to that. "This is the 2013 team. We want to always be competing. We want to win and win big." He mentioned to us again that the Hawks had gone undefeated through all four games of preseason only three times in history. And two of those times were when quarterback Russell Wilson was around. We all laughed. Then Coach added, "Every player on this team is valuable. Every one of you. I believe we've got what it takes this year to have the best season in Seahawks history."

No one dared whisper it, but you could see in the eyes of the players what every man in that room dreamed about. Coach was holding out for us the prospect of this team going all the way. He talked more about how we needed to bring the same hard-driving work ethic to every practice, to every game. From moment one, we needed to adopt a championship mindset. We were going out there to win. The Lombardi Trophy could be ours. We were only going to stop when we'd won it all.

If you're unfamiliar with the Seattle Seahawks, then you should know we're really a regional team, not just a city team. The fan base for the Hawks is huge and spread out over a large territory. The overall population in the Pacific Northwest isn't as densely packed as the East Coast, and some of the western states don't have an NFL team at all. Because of that, the Seahawks draw fans from as far away as Oregon to the south, from Idaho and Montana to the east, from Alaska way up in the ice and cold, and even from British Columbia and Alberta, the two westernmost provinces in Canada.

Seahawks fans—known collectively by the famous nickname "12th Man"—are nuts. (Eleven players from a team are on the field at any one time, so the fans are the "twelfth man" in the sense they can help out the team they cheer for.) I mean, Seattle fans are absolutely nuts in the best way possible. They've literally set a Guinness World Record for generating the loudest crowd noise at a sporting event. Previously it was held by a Turkish soccer club. The Seahawks set the new record, then the Kansas City Chiefs fans broke it to claim the distinction, then the Seahawks fans fought to take it back again—and won.

That resolve and fighting attitude dominates the region. By the start of 2013, the Seahawks had played for thirty-eight seasons, and even though our fan base is so utterly rabid, the fans had been deprived of the one thing every fan wants most—a Super Bowl victory. The 2005 Hawks came close when they beat the Panthers to win the NFC championship, but they did not win the Super Bowl that season (the game was played on February 5, 2006). The Steelers did, 21–10.

We've had our share of legendary players throughout the years, too. Steve Largent, Cortez Kennedy, and Warren Moon have all been inducted into the Pro Football Hall of Fame. Jim Zorn, Curt Warner (not to be confused with Kurt Warner, who I mentioned earlier), Dave Brown, Jacob Green, Dave Krieg, Matt Hasselbeck, Kenny Easley—these are household names with football-loving families around America.

This team was going to be my home, hopefully for a good long while. I couldn't wait for our first regular season game to begin.

We flew to North Carolina for our first game, against the Carolina Panthers, September 8, 2013. My parents flew out for that game, as did one of my agents, Derrick Fox, and I was able to connect with them all before the game started.

When I ran out onto the field and felt the roar in the stadium, it dawned on me. This moment—this was my dream come true. The day had finally arrived—I was going to play at least one snap in a regular game. I wasn't sitting on the sidelines, either. I was on all of the various special teams units—for kickoff, punts, and field goals. And I was starting as fullback. But I wasn't letting anything go to my head. I knew I needed to go out there and prove that they'd made the right decision, and that I wasn't there by default. Still, the moment was glorious.

In the game against Carolina, we had a couple of factors against us from the start. Kickoff began at 10 a.m., and with the three-hour time change from West to East Coast it was really our 7 a.m., which nobody on our team felt good about. The temperature was in the high eighties with a killer humidity, completely foreign to folks from Washington State. I said screw it and shook it all out of my mind. On the first run I ran as hard as I could and hit the first guy I saw as hard as possible. I wanted to let the Panthers know it was going to be a long day for them.

Both our offense and defense played strong all day. Going into the fourth quarter we were behind 7–6, but Russell Wilson was throwing off the hook. Any game that a quarterback can get over 300 yards is a good game, and I think Russell threw for something like 320 yards that day. I got three catches for 33 yards. That felt good, just to touch the ball in my first regular game. We took over toward the middle of the fourth quarter and ended up winning 12–7. The Seahawks were 1-0.

On the plane ride back, Tom Cable, the assistant head coach and offensive line coach, told me I had played a real good game. Coach Cable is old-school and aggressive, a real blood-in-the-mouth guy with a long history around professional football. He knew what he was talking about and never handed out compliments for free. I felt a bit of relief after he said that. All I needed to do was keep up that same level of intensity for the rest of the season.

The next week, September 15, we were up against the 49ers. Game day was Coach Pete Carroll's sixty-second birthday, and we wanted to give him the best present possible.

The Seahawks and the 49ers have a crazy rivalry, one of the biggest in all the NFL. San Francisco had gone to the Super Bowl the year before, and the 49ers were known for having a particularly brutal defense with well-known linebackers—like the quick-hitting Aldon Smith (265 pounds) and seasoned veteran Ahmad Brooks (259 pounds), to name two. We knew that if we could succeed against the 49ers, something was really clicking with our team.

Before the start of the game, I tried not think about the pressure on us that day. I knew I still needed to work on my technique as fullback. I was still amped up from our first win, and I consoled myself by thinking that even if I did something wrong in this next game, all wasn't lost. Sometimes plays can still be turned from mistakes, and I was going to give a 100 percent effort. Hey—I didn't expect the game to be easy. This was football—what did I think I'd signed up for anyway?

We got off to a good start. It was a home game at CenturyLink

Field. One of the craziest things was that the Seattle sky was black and stormy at kickoff. It was windy and rainy, and after a while of the storm not letting up, the game was actually delayed for an hour due to lightning. The Seattle fans kept their roar going anyway through the whole delay of game. Team members headed into the locker room during the delay and got a chance to adjust things, but I was thinking we just need to hurry up and get back out there. We didn't come this far to be delayed by lightning.

The storm blew over, the game continued, and we ended up whupping the crap out of San Francisco, 29–3. It was a great birthday present for Coach Carroll.

After the game, running back coach Sherman Smith walked over to me and told me that in only two games I'd improved to a degree it takes some guys a whole year to reach. "I'm saying this because you can handle it," he added. That helped raise my confidence. I knew then that I was on the team because of skill, not by default.

The next week was another home game, this time against Jacksonville. I didn't want to become comfortable with what Coach Smith had told me. We were 20-point favorites against the Jaguars, who were near the bottom of the rankings. But the Jags fought hard that day, and Russell Wilson got sacked twice in the first half. Our offense played well as a whole and we ended up winning 45–17, but there was a feeling as a team that we could have done better. If we wanted to go all the way, then we couldn't play as sloppy as we'd just done. Personally, I wasn't too happy with my performance.

On September 29, we flew to Houston to take on the Texans, the defending AFC South champions. There was a lot of talk in the press about how we'd never broken the 4-0 barrier before, so the pressure was on to win this game and prove everybody wrong.

Man, that was a gritty game right from the start. Hitting. Smacking. Pounding. Just a dogfight. Russell was getting killed in the first quarter by the Texans' defense, and everybody was worried late in the first half when our defensive lineman Michael Bennett took an absolutely brutal hit and went down like a rock. He's a huge veteran, six foot four and 275 pounds, and they needed to carry him out on a stretcher. (Fortunately, he recovered and came back a few games later.) At the half, we were down 20–3.

It wasn't until the beginning of the fourth quarter that we started to see any traction. Russell hit Doug Baldwin for a solid 24 yards. At first it was ruled incomplete by officials, but Coach Carroll challenged the call, and after review it was reversed. That became the game-changing play, and after that Russell just seemed to find his groove. He threw and scrambled and threw and scrambled, and we were back on the board. Our offense did great. Our defense did great. If we kept going, I knew this might turn into one of the greatest comebacks in Seahawk history. With less than eight minutes to go, Marshawn Lynch finished off that early fourth-quarter drive with a touchdown. Steven Hauschka kicked the extra point, making the score 20–13 for the Texans.

With around six minutes to go, we had the ball again, but Russell's pass to Jermaine Kearse was intercepted by the Texans, and Houston took over possession. It would be a huge battle for us to come back now, and our defense would need to come through big-time. Well, the defense did. A couple of plays later, Richard Sherman intercepted a pass and ran 58 yards for a touchdown. The kick was good, which tied the teams at 20 and sent the game into overtime.

A couple of plays into OT we were backed up deep and needed to hit hard to get any forward traction. The only thing that went through my mind was "hit the first thing you see." The ball was snapped. I don't even know who my guy was, I just pushed hard past him, hit the next guy, and kept going. A hole was clear, and I think it was Marshawn again who plowed ahead to gain long yardage. All the way I helped lead block for him. That felt good.

We ended up winning in overtime, 23–20. It wasn't a great game, but we were doing what we needed to do. We were going out every day, every practice, every game, and pushing as hard as we could. And for the first time in Seahawks' history we were 4-0!

We played the Indianapolis Colts on October 6. It was an away game, and I was made honorary captain, but it wasn't a good day for me or anyone else. It's all sort of a blur now. We missed touchdown opportunities three times in the third quarter and had to settle for field goals. We lost the game 34–28 and went to 4-1.

On October 13 we played a home game against the Tennessee Titans. Most of my friends from California came up for that game. They were confident company, and it felt great to have some home team support like that. It helped me play better. I was remembering hanging out with them in the good old days at Troy High School when we used to murder other teams. I had a strong tackle in the Tennessee game as well as a fumble recovery, but it was overturned. At the end, we won the game 20–13, but it was a less than perfect win.

In our running-back room at the facility, there's a bucketful of money. If you fumble and don't recover, it costs you a thousand bucks. Dropped passes are understood, and they're only twenty bucks. But fumbles are big deals, and I owed money to the pot after that game due to a fumble that went out of bounds. It took me a couple of days afterward to collect the money and deliver. Another player said, "Dude, where your presidents at?" And I was like, "Dude, they're still chilling at the bank."

October 17 was an away game against the Arizona Cardinals. It was one day before my twenty-third birthday, and I had a good game. My blocking was on point. But toward the end of the second quarter I caught a pass on a flat route and felt a *pop, pop, pop* in my upper hamstring. Never having had an injury like that, I thought it was a cramp at first and limped over to the sidelines, where the trainers had me lie on my stomach, put my legs up, and try to pull my foot down. Nothing was happening. It was a pulled hamstring for sure.

The injury didn't hurt too bad, and I figured I'd be okay soon enough. I was the only fullback on the roster, and sometimes you can move the tight end to the fullback position, but it's not quite the same. We beat the Cardinals 34–22, so that was good, but I was noticing that every time I sat down, my leg hurt real bad. The next day I went to get an MRI, and they told me it was a pretty bad tear after all, right where the ham and glute meet. The tear was a little less than an inch away from the bone, which was the only good news that day. You most definitely don't want to tear your hamstring to the bone, because that means surgery.

Instead they did plasma injections on me. They draw blood from your arm, put it in a machine and take the good stuff out, then inject that good stuff back into you at the point of the tear. I was going to be out for a while. The team still kept me on active roster, which was a blessing. But I was concerned because just then they decided to bring Michael Robinson back up. He was feeling better, so they re-signed him to a one-year contract on October 22. How do you like that? When he got hurt, I came in, and then when I got hurt, he came back in. That's how football can go.

I sat out the next game with the Rams, which we won 19–9, and the next game after that with Tampa Bay, which we squeaked by in overtime, 27–24. Then I sat out the Atlanta game, which we won 33–10, and the Vikings game, which we won 41–20. The next week was what they call a "bye," meaning a week off for the whole team, so that bought me another week's time to heal. I'll tell ya, it was hard to not be playing in the games. I was going to rehab and I still went to team meetings, but it was frustrating. I came to be on the field, not to watch.

I came back for the December 2 game against the New Orleans Saints. It was on *Monday Night Football*, nationally televised, and I wasn't going to miss this for the world. Another teammate had strained his hamstring the same time as me, which is a simpler injury compared to the tear that I had. He and I both came back the same time—that's how bad I wanted to be back in.

Since I'd sat out those four games, Michael Robinson was now starting fullback, and I was backing him up. Altogether I was the third running back on the team and the second fullback, so that meant I was mainly playing on special teams. It was tempting to think I was at the back of the line again, but this game against the Saints would prove something else entirely.

The game was important for a lot of reasons. We'd been keeping competitors at bay all season long, and the Saints were our closest competitors. We had a two-game lead on them, and if we beat them, we'd be way up in the standings and in prime position for the playoffs. We hadn't clinched the NFC West yet, meaning the playoffs weren't a guarantee, but the reality of us being in the playoffs was getting closer by the minute.

The game started strongly. Russell threw calmly and with deadly force. He threw a 60-yard pass to Zach Miller and a 52-yarder to Doug Baldwin. Time and time again we moved up the field to score. Hauschka had two field goals. We were ahead 27–7 at the half.

In the third quarter we plowed up the field only to be stopped right before the Saints' end zone. It was second down and goal. I think we were only eight yards away. Russell took the snap, back-pedaled, and pumped it hard to tight end Kellen Davis. It looked a little high, and I followed the ball as it bounced off Davis's head and into the air. I said, "Ooooh, ball," and snagged it coming down. Two quick steps later I dove into the end zone. It all happened so fast. A lot of players were around me, and I wasn't quite sure what the call was. I looked around for the nearest referee and saw that several refs had come together to talk it over. Then the call was made. Two hands in the air.

Touchdown!

Again, I didn't visibly celebrate the moment or anything. Teammates high-fived me, but that was it. The game was still on. The next play was what mattered. There was more work to be done. In the end, we beat the Saints 34–7, and Coach Carroll called it a great game. That's where more of the celebration began.

My teammates said later that I looked natural when I got that touchdown, but I honestly had no idea what the heck happened. It didn't matter. Man, you score a touchdown in a regular season game and something changes in how the 12th Man perceives you. My notoriety went from zero to sixty in a hurry. People started saying things like, "Wait a minute—isn't that the dude who can't hear? He scored a touchdown!" People texted me right and left. They were saying the blogosphere was lighting up, talking about me. I tried to keep it all in good stride and not pay much attention to it. If you've got buzz about you, then you need to know that buzz is going to come and go, so don't concern yourself about the buzz. Your job is to play the game. For me, the season wasn't over yet, and we still had a lot of work to do.

Those last four games of the regular season are a blur now. We lost to the San Francisco 49ers, 17–19, then clobbered the New York Giants, 23–0. Then we lost to the Arizona Cardinals, 10–17, and beat the St. Louis Rams, 27–9.

The regular season was over. We had gone 13-3 and were in first place in the NFC West, and we'd clinched home-field advantage throughout the upcoming playoffs. It seemed like everywhere you went in Seattle, there was Seahawks gear. I mean everywhere. Walk into a mall or a restaurant and everybody was wearing Seahawks shirts and hats. We were headed to the divisional playoffs, and the whole region was amped up, looking forward to what was well within reach.

It was an incredible time to be on the Seahawks team, and there were times it was hard to believe that this was my first full season of playing in the NFL. It felt like I'd been waiting for such a long time, then suddenly accelerated to freeway speed, all in a rush.

But something else big would happen right around the play-offs. It would happen to me personally, and forever change how I saw being in the back of the line.

14

GOING VIRAL IN THE PLAYOFFS

Back in the regular season, about a week before the Rams game, I had gotten a call from a media guy representing Duracell batteries. They'd contacted the Seahawks and the information had been forwarded to my agent, who set up a meeting. At first I wasn't sure of what they were asking. I had a pack of Duracell batteries right there in my locker. They were my favorite brand, and the company officials were asking me to be in a commercial. I figured the project was going to be pretty small, but that didn't bother me. Seriously—the only thing I thought I'd get out of it was some free batteries. Hey, I could always use those.

The shoot for the commercial was scheduled for New Year's Eve, 2013. It was going to take all day. The night before, I'd allowed myself to enjoy a rare late night out with some friends who were up from California. We'd gotten back at two in the morning. A car service was picking me up at 6 a.m. So I got a couple hours' sleep, woke up and got in the car when it came, then slept all the way from my apartment to the stadium.

All this equipment was already set up there by the time I arrived, but I wasn't giving it much notice. First thing I did was go get coffee—three of them—and I rarely drink coffee, but I was gathering that this was going to be a long day. Man, as soon as it was in my system, I wondered what ever came over me to drink all that coffee. The caffeine ran through my system. I started shaking, and there was no way to exercise and let out all the nervousness.

They filmed me a bunch in the stadium, then we went to another location and they filmed me in a bus, then we went to the practice facility at the University of Washington and they filmed me there, and then to a neighborhood to get some shots of me running. I got home at ten o'clock that night, New Year's Eve. You know what I did for New Year's Eve that year? I slept!

On New Year's Day, January 1, 2014, we needed to go back to a recording studio and do the voice-over for the script. The guy who wrote it, Lincoln Boehm—we totally hit it off, and I'm still in contact with him today. The script was great; I felt like a rapper making an album, and I probably said each line twenty different times, twenty different ways, so they could get the perfect sound and mix it all together. I had that script memorized by the end. It's still embedded in my brain.

I got a bit of money for doing the commercial, and a year's worth of Duracell batteries—and when I heard about the year's worth of batteries I was like, *Yes!* because I was buying my own batteries by then, not my parents. So that was worth a lot right there. I grasped that there was a bigger reason for doing the commercial, too, although its full impact didn't dawn on me right away. Sure, I hoped to inspire people with the commercial, particularly children who are perhaps facing bullying or some obstacle they need to overcome. My big message was for them to trust the power within and achieve their dreams.

I mean, every kid faces some sort of challenge growing up. Every kid. For me, when it came to playing football, I needed to prove to other folks that I was just like them, that I belonged. I needed to prove that I was just as good as everybody else. My Duracell commercial was telling people to believe in their dreams—and that was a message I could grasp with my whole heart. Nobody's perfect. Everybody has something to overcome. Everybody has an opportunity to do what they want to do. You have to go for your goal even though it's going to take a long time to get there. Even if you don't get there, make sure you've done everything you can in that direction. The only person who can say no to you is God, and He wouldn't put an opportunity in your sight if He didn't know you could handle it.

After that, I pretty much forgot about the commercial. I wasn't sure what it would do or when it would be aired. There are a lot of TV channels these days, tons, really, so it's pretty easy for one commercial to get buried under all the noise. I pretty much put it out of my mind. Little did I know that commercial was going to be anything but small.

We went to the divisional playoffs on January 11. We were playing the New Orleans Saints. It was raining hard that day in Seattle. But we didn't care about the weather. You get this championship mentality. You get confident. You can play through any storm.

I'd broken up with my girlfriend right before that. I respected her a lot, but it wasn't going to work out long-term, so I was feeling down. My friends Brandon, Dani, and Derek flew up to Seattle, and it was good to see them. They cheered me up, and we had some fun before the game. That helped me overcome that rough spot.

The Saints game began, and right away it was a dogfight. It was hard even to watch the game. The action went back and forth, back and forth. We were up 16–0 at halftime, which is way better than being down 16–0 at the half, but even so, we felt shaky. No game is finished at halftime, and they were still hitting us hard.

Near the end of the third quarter, the Saints had the ball and marched down the field, play after play, and on the fourth play of the fourth quarter they punched through for a touchdown. Instead of going for one point after, they attempted a two-point conversion and got it. That cut our lead by half, 16–8, so things still felt uneasy. The Saints burned their time-outs—two the regular way. Then they challenged a catch that Doug Baldwin made from Russell, but lost the challenge, which meant they also lost their third and final time-out. With about four minutes to go, I started to breathe easier. It was still our possession, and Marshawn ran hard off the left end for a 31-yard touchdown, which put us ahead 23–8. After that came a couple more hard hits, and a couple more passes. They scored again, 23–15. With thirty-two seconds left, the Saints attempted an onside kick and recovered the ball. The pressure was on, big-time. Thankfully, time ran out and we won the game. I let out a huge sigh of relief.

But this was also big news: I didn't find out until *after* the game that they'd played my commercial right before the start of it. I mean, this was no ordinary game—it was the divisional playoffs. How many people were tuned in? It had to be a ton. All the players were in the tunnel when they showed the commercial, and I didn't see it. In fact, I hadn't even seen the final mix yet. They showed it to the whole stadium—and right away it was already all over YouTube, too. It turned out to be one of those mega-ads, and it was everywhere. People were texting me left and right saying things like, "Man, I cried when I saw your commercial."

You gotta realize that I didn't even have a Twitter or Facebook account at the time. I wanted my life to stay private. But that wasn't going to happen. Right after the Duracell ad blew up, I got a Twitter account so I could be with the fans who were reaching out. The first mistake I made with Twitter was asking Richard Sherman to give me a shout-out to get fans, because he was hot already. He tweeted something and my phone went berserk. I hadn't yet turned off my email notifications, and my phone died in just two minutes. I had fifteen thousand emails. It took me an hour to deactivate the notifications and get rid of all that. Everybody started writing me. I mean everybody. I responded to as many messages as I could, but I still wasn't realizing how big this thing had gotten. America took this commercial to another level.

Over the next week, the Duracell spot continued to go crazy. (As of the writing of this book, it's been viewed more than 22 million times.) People said they connected with it; it inspired them.

The commercial talks about how I was picked on as a kid, how people gave up on me, how they told me I should just quit. It traced back to how I wasn't picked for the NFL Draft, and how I was sure my dream was over. But the good news was that I wasn't listening to that—know what I mean? I wasn't listening because I was tuning out all that negative talk. Despite all those obstacles, I made it to the NFL anyway. I was even scoring touchdowns in the NFL. The fans in the NFL were cheering me on, and I could hear them all, loud and clear!

Because of that commercial, and because we'd gotten so far as a team, I started getting requests for interviews left and right. Right after the Saints game, I had four interviews—two at the facility, and two later on that evening at the hotel. These were like a half hour each. I wanted to go home and relax like I normally did, but those days were behind me. My agent coached me through it and told me to ride the wave. ABC's *Good Morning America* called after that. *People* magazine. More interviews came. And I was just thinking, *All right then, let's do this.*

My family were all proud of me—and a bit protective, too. We had people calling us from Florida saying they'd seen the commercial. From Washington. From the Northeast. From all over Los Angeles. It was bigger than we'd ever thought it would be. My mom and dad both advised me that when fame comes to a person, there are often people who come along with that fame, and sometimes not all of them have your best interests in mind, or they just want to use your fame for their own purposes. But my mom and dad helped me strike a good balance there, I'd say. It was a proud moment for us all.

The second round of playoffs, the NFC Championship game, was set for January 19. The winner of this game would go to the Super Bowl. We were set to play the San Francisco 49ers, and it was that big rivalry again, the exact matchup that a lot of people wanted to see. In the history of us playing them, the teams were tied at 15 wins. Exactly matched. It was the ultimate showdown to see who'd go all the way.

That week the Seahawks were on the cover of *Sports Illustrated.* Some people thought that would jinx us, but even as superstitious as I can sometimes be, I wasn't letting that bother me. As a team we were in great shape. We had the Beast mentality, and we were going to drive as hard as we possibly could.

The game began, and the play itself was very intense, maybe the most intense I've ever been in. It felt like we were back at Troy and playing against La Habra, our biggest rival, or when I was at UCLA and we played Arizona State my senior year. It was a dog-fight right from the start. I had a good tackle right on kickoff, but it was hard after that for us to get much traction. Russell got hit hard on the first play and the ball came loose. The 49ers recovered it on our fifteen-yard line. Play after play went like that, back and forth, and it didn't take long before they were up 10–0. Wilson got sacked four times in the first half, and when we went into the locker room, it was a seven-point game.

I hate the idea of big suspense. For example, I love Christmas because it's Jesus's birthday, but I hate waiting to unwrap presents under the tree. Man, the second half of that game was all about suspense. Marshawn got a strong run, which tied the game at 10–10. But the 49ers scored right after that to pull ahead again by seven. Russell connected with Jermaine Kearse to even the score. Back and forth, back and forth, fumbles, hard hits, nobody could predict the outcome. It all came down to the final drive. The 49ers quarterback, Colin Kaepernick, took the snap and threw a hard strike meant for Michael Crabtree. But Richard Sherman jumped up into the air, twisted like nobody's business, and swatted the ball away. Malcolm Smith grabbed the interception in the end zone and we had the ball. Everybody cheered like mad. The stadium shook. It all happened so fast, I needed to watch the play again on replay to see what happened.

It was true. The game was over. We won, 23–17. We were going to the Super Bowl. It was hard to process that thought. The Super Bowl.

I mean . . . THE SUPER BOWL!

After the Denver Broncos won the AFC title game over the New England Patriots and the final matchup was set, there was a two-week wait for the Super Bowl. And I found a lot could get packed into those two weeks.

I mentioned how I was getting a lot of mail around then. One letter came after the 49ers game from a nine-year-old girl named Riley Kovalcik. She and her twin sister, Erin, had seen my commercial, and with her dad's permission, Riley had written to me.

Her dad sent me the letter. Both the girls are hearing impaired, and Riley's letter said in part,

> I know how you feel. I also have hearing aids. Just try your best. I have faith in you. I love sports. Go Seattle Seahawks.

She went on to talk about what we had in common. And I guess something about that little letter really stood out to me. I don't know exactly what it was. She was encouraging me on, I guess. I was telling her that anything could be done, even with a disability, and she was saying right back to me, Yep, you know it, Derrick. You can do anything if you put your mind to it.

It was a really busy time for us as a team. Every day the Seahawks had meetings in the morning, then we had a walk-through, then lunch, then practice. One morning I had ten minutes free, so I sat down in the players' lounge and wrote Riley and Erin back. I didn't do it to be public. They weren't asking me for anything. It was just to let them know they weren't alone, and to encourage them to do great, too. After I sent my letter, their father, Jake, wrote me back and said, "You have no clue how much this means to them. I know you're busy with #SuperBowl prep & truly appreciate the note!"

That's all I ever thought would happen. It was just one of many notes that fans wrote to me during that season. But, man, I hadn't realized yet how public this world is these days. Word of that small exchange got out, and the next thing you know it's on Fox Sports, ABC News, *Washington Post*—the story just made the rounds. There's more to this story, too—just hang on, I'll tell you in a minute.

We had a hard week of practice, then we got ready as a team to travel to New Jersey for the Super Bowl. This is kinda funny, but before we left, I realized I needed some new clothes. Plenty of players will dress up real nice before and after a game, but I've never been one of them. I just think, *Well, all that I'm going to do is get in my car, drive over to the facility, and walk about fifty yards from the parking lot inside and then change, so why bother with the fancy clothes?* Know what I mean? I'm going to wear something comfortable. But the Super Bowl was different. So I went to Men's Wearhouse and got a couple of suits so I at least had something nice to wear.

We flew to New Jersey, then had another week there before the game. When we first walked into the lobby of the hotel we were staying at, there was Super Bowl stuff everywhere—signs, posters, banners. I was as excited as a little kid, taking pictures of every-thing. I knew that getting to the Super Bowl is an extremely rare opportunity. There are guys who've been playing in the league their whole lives—and playing well—who never get the chance to go to the Super Bowl, so I wasn't going to waste this opportunity for anything.

During the days we had practice, but practice wasn't as hard as before—80 percent, probably. The real work had been done during the regular season. Now it was mostly mental preparation. Coach didn't want anybody getting injured before the big game. I mean, every game during the regular season that we play, we treat it like the Super Bowl. We go as hard out as we can. All that work was under our belts. Now we just needed to connect and make the big game happen.

Around the second day we were in New Jersey, my agent called and said that the twins who'd written to me, Riley and Erin, were getting interviewed in a nearby hotel, and would I mind coming over and surprising them? Their family lives in New Jersey, so their house wasn't far away. I said sure. So I showed up. Their mom and dad were there, along with their younger brother, Aiden. They weren't expecting me at all, and I popped around the corner and said hello and personally thanked the girls for their support. It was pretty cool to see the surprise in their eyes.

"Oh my gosh, are you real?" Erin said when she saw me.

I invited them to the Super Bowl, along with their parents and little brother, and handed them tickets. They were pretty good tickets, too, not far from the field.

The girls were stunned. Picture Disneyland and Christmas all rolled into one. They were both grinning, and I think they only said two words at first. "Really?" and "Seriously?" Then they hugged me and said thank you. I hugged them right back. It was a pretty cool moment all around, and it was hard not to get a tear in your eye. I think their dad was about to cry, too. We all talked a bit and we took some pictures and just hung out for a while. I wish them and their whole family well to this day.

What's funny is that my friend Brian is originally from New Jersey, and his dad lives about five houses down from where the Kovalciks live. What a small world.

A bunch of my friends from California flew in for the game. It was great to have them there. My parents and sister came, along with some other relatives. It felt like a whole bunch of family was supporting me in a big way.

That whole week before the big game was nonstop activity. We had more practices and a media day. I hit up Lincoln, who lives in New Jersey and who wrote the script for the Duracell commercial, and we went to a Brooklyn Nets basketball game one evening, which was a lot of fun. I went to a Knicks game the next night with my agent. One of my longtime friends, Hillary, had moved to Brooklyn, so the next evening we connected and got a cab and hung out with her roommates, then we all went to a sports bar and shot some pool.

One of my old teammates from Troy High School, Aaron Brewer, was playing for the Broncos, so we tried to meet up but kept missing each other. Another Bronco, Ronny Hillman, had gone to La Habra High School, our biggest rival, so three players from the same area were now playing in the Super Bowl.

Media day was crazy. I asked Marshawn what to expect, and all he said was "I'm all about the action." Whatever that meant, it proved pretty much right. You've got all these media people coming from everywhere. I talked to reporters from South America, Australia—and all over the United States. The whole world is interested in the Super Bowl. With all the accents that were being spoken that day, I wondered if some of those reporters could understand what I was saying.

The actress Alyssa Milano was hosting a party in the evening after media day, and I went to it. For years I'd seen her in *Who's the Boss*, and I had been watching her new series, *Mistresses*. The Super Bowl parties are supposed to be for the players, but when I saw her, I was starstruck. I didn't know what to say. We talked a bit, and took some pictures, and I just kept smiling, looking at her.

Two days before the Super Bowl, my agent told me a story about a ten-year-old hearing-impaired boy named Jack Coleman, who was a huge fan and doing everything he could to find a Seahawks No. 40 jersey with "Coleman" on the back. So far, he couldn't find one, since stores on the East Coast typically don't stock as much material from teams on the West Coast, even if the players are in the Super Bowl. I guess Jack had been a die-hard New York Giants fan all his life, but when he saw my commercial, he'd switched his favorite team to the Hawks. So I thought that was pretty cool.

The owner of the Modell's Sporting Goods chain contacted my agent and told him they could find the boy a jersey. So my agent asked me if I could stop by the Modell's store in Times Square and meet the boy and give him his jersey in person. I said sure. It took a while to get there because of traffic. This was Friday night in New York.

They were all waiting at the store—Jack, his parents, and younger sisters—and they'd been there a long time. I heard later that nobody had told the little boy what he was doing there—they wanted it to be a big surprise. Anyway, when I got there, I crept up from around a corner and surprised them. I still remember their faces when I appeared. Jack looked like he'd just seen Santa Claus. My agent had tears in his eyes—and he never cries. The dad walked away and started crying. It was one of those moments where a dad is feeling something strong for his son. He knows his son is going to have some hard times in life, but maybe this bit of encouragement will help him get through some of them. I gave Jack a signed football that said, "Stay strong, stay cool, have fun!!!" And a jersey with "Coleman" on the back. Definitely a good moment.

A couple of months later, my agent got an email from the boy's mom. The family was taking a vacation to Glacier National Park in Montana, and they were thinking about heading out to Seattle to watch a preseason game. They did come to Seattle and I hung out with them a bit then, too. They watched a practice, and I asked if they'd like to come by the next day for a tour of the facility. So we did that. It was good to see the family again.

Another evening right before the Super Bowl, I went to Gallaudet University, which is located in Washington, D.C., and is for deaf and hard of hearing students. They've got a football program there, and I met with some of the students and hung out. A big ole lineman talked to me for a while, and told me that basically I'd opened the door for all of them. He was very thankful. I didn't quite know what to say—I don't think about what I've done that way. Basically, I just wanted to play football, so I found a way to play. But he was telling me that we needed to prove to people that hearing aids won't hold anybody back. I tried to encourage him to keep on going, keep working hard, keep doing his thing.

The night before the Super Bowl game, I didn't do anything big. Me and my friends from California grabbed dinner at this random Italian place near the hotel. I think the nerves were starting to hit a bit by then, because the whole week had been a blur of activity and meeting people and practicing and living in the moment. I was trying not to think about the game much, but enjoying every second of this experience.

I remember well how Derek M. put things into perspective. We were all sitting at the table and he said in my direction, "Regardless of the outcome of tomorrow's game, you need to realize where you came from, who you started with, and what chances people gave you. They gave you zero chances, and now you've succeeded. You've already won over everybody. You've overcome all these obstacles, all the things that were said against you. Regardless of what happens tomorrow, you will always be the Derrick Coleman Jr. we know and love. The things you've done, we're so proud of you. We knew that someday this would be your path in life."

I was on the verge of tears when he said that. Yeah, I was. Tomorrow was the biggest game of my life, but I knew that in the eyes of my friends nothing was going to change. That meant a lot to me. It sure did.

15

THE SUPER BOWL

The morning of Sunday, February 2, 2014, arrived. I had that new suit with me, so I got up and put that on to be looking good. When the first bus left the Westin hotel in Jersey City where we stayed to head over to MetLife Stadium in East Rutherford, New Jersey, I was on it.

On the ride over, I was doing the same thing I always do, trying to think of this day as just another game. We needed to go as hard as we possibly could; we needed to give it our all. I was listening to music with my headphones on, working to enter the Beast zone. Whenever I listen to music, I can't understand the words off the bat. I listen for the beat. The music's got to be absolutely cranked for me to hear anything. For me, full volume is someone else's barely on volume. I listen with my hearing aids in, and I like over-the-ear headphones, never in-the-ear. If I listen to a song over and over again, then I can start picking up words. Sometimes I go online and look up the lyrics to understand what they're saying, and sometimes that's too bad, because I'll like the beat of a song but then I'll find out what the words are and I don't like the song anymore. I don't remember what I was listening to that day. Something loud. Something blasting.

The bus I was on arrived forty-five minutes early, which is the way I liked it. At the stadium, I did what I always do—changed, got into workout clothes, and found a special conditioning coach. Back when I was on practice squad, I'd do this same little workout every day—some running, some stretching, some arms, some core—nothing crazy, just a tiny workout. And that worked for me. So when I made it onto the team, I kept up that same little workout routine. The one time I didn't do that workout was the time I pulled my hamstring. So today of all days I didn't want to jinx anything.

After the workout I played catch a bit with some of my teammates, just waiting. Then I took a shower. I like to be clean, and I'll often take a shower before a game as well as afterward. On the day of the Super Bowl, a lot's going on, and I knew there would be a lot of waiting this day, killing time. You've got to keep your mind busy or else you'll go nuts. After my shower I toweled off, put my pads on, and suited up in my uniform. I did all the same routines then, too. Put on my jersey a certain way. Taped my wrists a certain way. Marshawn's locker was right next to mine, and he had these big speakers out and was blasting music. He was doing his pregame routine, a lot of crazy dancing and singing.

Then it was time to go out and warm up as a team, the same thing we do every game. The adrenaline was really starting to kick in at that point. Walking out on that field—it's hard to explain the feeling that came over me. I knew that this day was absolutely huge. It was like this excited rush you get when you know something good's about to happen. Once I did the first pass in warm-ups, the rush diminished. Everything felt normal, and I was back in the groove, doing the same routines I'd always been doing.

After the warm-up, we all headed back into the locker room and waited again. I tried to stay in the zone, tried to keep my mind occupied. I got the quarterback play sheet and went over it one last time, rehearsing each play in my mind. I wanted to be dead sure I knew every play cold—and knew it instantly. I wanted to have my mind locked in so there was no guesswork involved.

Game time came around. Everybody got up and we prayed in the locker room, like we do before each game. Coach said some words, and we got ready to walk out. I was feeling what I feel normally, excited, but more so this time. I knew it was a blessing to be able to go out there and do what I loved to do.

We ran through the tunnel. We were all hyped up then. We burst out into the stadium. Man, I've been in big stadiums before, including the MetLife to play the Giants. But this day was different. Everything was amped up. Everything was bigger. There were more than eighty-two thousand people inside the stadium, screaming, going nuts. Not only that, but more people were watching this Super Bowl on TV than ever before in history. More than 111.5 million people would watch the game in the United States alone. Millions more around the world would tune in, too. I knew that my Grandma Coleman was having a Super Bowl party at her house in L.A. She had fifty people over and two big-screen TVs hooked up. It was a full house of celebrating, and Grandma had cooked up spaghetti and fried chicken, hot wings, green salad, and French rolls with garlic spread.

Announcers were calling this the perfect Super Bowl matchup. We'd finished the regular season 13-3 and won the NFC West division, earning home-field advantage throughout the NFC playoffs. Denver had also finished their regular season 13-3, and had won the AFC West division, earning home-field advantage throughout the AFC playoffs. Both our offenses and defenses were explosive and tough. Peyton Manning, quarterback for the Broncos, was a sixteen-year veteran of the NFL and had won a Super Bowl ring in 2007 when he played for the Indianapolis Colts. Russell Wilson, our quarterback, was a relative newcomer, having been in the NFL only since 2012. At five feet eleven inches, he was considered too small to play in the NFL. But he'd proved everybody wrong and was strong, quick, and hungry.

I stood on the sidelines and watched and listened as Queen Latifah sang "America the Beautiful" as the last part of the pregame show. Opera singer Renée Fleming then sang the national anthem. About halfway through, I glanced up at the big screen, and they were showing a picture of me. There was a picture of a woman next to me using sign language to sign the national anthem, and I couldn't help but chuckle, because I wondered if they knew I don't sign. It didn't matter. After the anthem was over, I saluted, like I always do in honor of our troops. Military planes and helicopters flew overhead. Football legends Joe Namath and Phil Simms did the coin toss. We won the toss and deferred, meaning we'd kick off to the Broncos to start the first half.

Then it was time for kickoff. I ran out onto the field as part of special teams. More adrenaline was coursing through me than I've ever felt. I remember exactly what it felt like when our kicker, Steven Hauschka, set the ball down on the tee. It was like I woke up. I was still in a dream more amazing than I could ever imagine, but I was seeing everything with a new clarity. Hauschka kicked the ball, and I charged downfield.

Trindon Holliday caught the ball for the Broncos deep in the end zone and started to sprint forward. That was a bad decision. Two big guys were in front of Trindon, blocking me. I hit one of them hard. My head snapped back. He felt like a brick wall. I caught myself and kept running. Trindon was coming my way and I dove out and got to him first, holding him up. Number 20, Jeremy Lane, from our team grabbed Trindon, too, and together we got the first tackle on the twelve-yard line. A good way to begin the game.

The first play after that—you had to look twice to believe it happened. Peyton Manning called for the snap, but I think it was too loud in the stadium for him to hear because he started to walk forward like he was going to repeat himself to the center or maybe change the play. The ball went back anyway, high over Peyton's head, and bounced into our end zone. We got a safety—two points—and were on the scoreboard within twelve seconds of the game's start, the fastest score in Super Bowl history.

Honestly, I couldn't tell you much of what happened the rest of the game. It was all such a blur. I was living in the moment, having so much crazy fun. I wish I could give you a play-by-play of it now, but the game sped by for me, and it's all an amazing mix of sights and images in my mind. People say that the Broncos fell apart, but I don't know about that. They played hard the whole way through, and we had our hands full.

By halftime, we were up 22–0 and had all the confidence in the world, but no one was celebrating in the locker room yet. We were still thinking the score was 0–0. That's how you need to play. Football games are only won in the fourth quarter, and plenty of teams have come from behind to win a game. Halftime at the Super Bowl takes longer than at a normal game, and the Red Hot Chili Peppers and Bruno Mars were performing, two bands I wanted to see. But we all just waited in the locker room, getting anxious before coming out on the field again. Finally halftime was over. We went back out onto the field and warmed up a bit. Then kept playing hard.

When did we know for certain we'd won? I'd say that going into the fourth quarter, we were all feeling pretty good. We scored a touchdown on the first drive of the quarter to make the score 43–8. Our defense was unstoppable, our offense commanding and calm. It was just straight playing then. A fun football game for us. We could always still blow it, of course, but if we kept up the dominant performance across the board like we were doing, then this game was going to be ours. With just over a minute left at the end of the fourth quarter, Russell Wilson and Zach Miller dumped the Gatorade on Coach Carroll, and the rest was history. The Seahawks were world champs for the first time ever!

Blue and green confetti started flying everywhere. It looked like a snowstorm. We were all yelling and running around going crazy. Commentators and reporters were down on the field. A huge Seahawks logo stood out on the overhead screens with the words "Champion" underneath. We were all getting interviewed. I saw my friends from California—somehow they'd gotten down onto the field. I saw my mom and dad and sister make their way down. It was just nuts.

We believed we could get here. Right from the start of the season, Coach knew we had the talent and heart to go all the way. We wanted to win it all and we did. We reached this destination. We were the champions.

We all lined up, and the Vince Lombardi Trophy came down the line for the official presentation. Lots of guys were kissing the trophy, but I didn't want to kiss it until after it went to the cleaners. We were celebrating like you always see teams do on TV, but this time it was different for me. This time I was in the middle of the celebration. I was part of it. It felt like anything was possible. Today was proof.

When the trophy ceremony was over, we showered and changed and got on the bus. Late in the evening of the Super Bowl was a huge party back at the hotel. My friends from California came and met us there. Paul Allen, the Seahawks owner, was in the room, smiling ear to ear and shaking hands all around. Everybody had his own bottle of champagne. People were dancing, enjoying themselves, eating good food, having fun.

After we partied for a while, there was talk of going somewhere else to continue the fun, but honestly, I was spent. I was thinking, *Everything is here, why should we go anywhere else?* Besides, it was the end of a long, long day, and I was tired.

We stayed the night in New Jersey, then the next morning hopped on a plane to go back to Seattle. There'd been talk earlier that New Jersey wasn't the best place to hold a Super Bowl, because it is a cold-weather site and anything can happen in the depths of winter. But the temperature for the game had stayed good at a relatively balmy 49 degrees. Overnight, a heavy snowstorm came up, and we sat on the runway for some time while they deiced the plane. We had the plane to ourselves, a charter. The coaches sit in first class. The media and staff sit in the middle. The players sit in the back.

When we arrived back in Seattle, a huge crowd was waiting for us. Normally it takes us about twenty minutes to get from the airport to the facility in Renton, but that day it took us more than an hour. The streets were filled. People were tapping the buses. Police escorts were on the freeway for us. People were cheering, shouting, putting their hands out of car windows. Some were standing up out of car sunroofs. It had been the same way when we'd left for New Jersey, too. A big sendoff. Now a big return.

A couple of days later, the city of Seattle held a huge parade for us. It was cold, and the parade started at the Space Needle and went to the stadium. We rode out in the open on the back of trucks, huddled together for body heat, and something like seven hundred thousand people showed up for the parade. It was crazy. People were piled way back in crowds on the sides of the road. People stood on the roofs of buildings. They leaned from windows and waved and cheered. Finally we made it to the stadium. It was packed, too. We took the stage and they presented us the trophy again. Coach said a few good words. All of us players were playing the fool in the background, poking teammates and having fun.

That was the official end. Right after that parade, I got in my car and started heading back to L.A. I drove for about three hours, then hit big snow in southern Oregon. Interstate 5 was closed, and no one was making it through. So I turned around and drove back to Seattle. The next morning I caught an early flight and went home that way.

What does a young man do after he's just won the Super Bowl?

Some go to Disneyland. I went to Fiji. Earlier, I'd planned to take a trip with my girlfriend, so the tickets were already bought. But since she wasn't in the picture anymore, I phoned up my good buddy Derek M. and asked if he wanted to go instead.

It was a long flight to Fiji, about eleven hours from L.A. Once there, we caught a smaller plane to one of the smaller islands. Then we got on a boat and headed another twenty minutes or so to a private island resort called Matangi. It was a romantic setting, something you'd put on your bucket list, for sure, but Derek and I didn't care. We went snorkeling, kayaking, and hiking. Every day we played volleyball in the afternoon. The trip wasn't so much to rest my body. My body felt fine, even after all the hits I'd taken during the regular season. The trip was to rest my mind. I needed a mental break from the intensity of football. Chandler Fenner and his girlfriend came and joined us after a few days, so we all had a good time together.

The people in Fiji had watched the Super Bowl and knew

who Chandler and I were. We toured an elementary school while we were there, because they'd asked us, and met with the kids to encourage them. I'd called Chandler earlier and told him to bring some candy and Seahawks shirts for the kids. Anything we could do to help. They were raising money to help get some programs off the ground, and we both donated to that. We played rugby with the kids afterward. Those little kids played hard. Man, some of them were just brutal.

We came home after about ten days, then I headed out to Las Vegas with some of my friends from home for a weekend of slots and fun. Nobody won any money, but we didn't care. That was the extent of my personal celebrations.

Back at home, there wasn't too much time to think. There were photo shoots and interviews with the press—one right after the other. It felt like there wasn't much off-season at all. The OTAs were coming up, and I needed to prepare for those. I kept training, lifting, and doing drills like I always did. I started speaking more at corporate events and went to Florida to speak at a Duracell convention, then did a second trip to speak at the American Academy of Audiology. I met lots of friendly people everywhere I went. I did some work with Starkey hearing aids. I spoke at a few more schools and did a few community outreach events.

I'd often watched the hit ABC TV show *Switched at Birth* and loved it. If you've never seen it before, it features several hard-of-hearing characters. One of the show's producers and I got connected through Twitter, and they had me do a cameo on an episode. I wasn't thinking I had a future career in acting or anything. It was just fun. Hopefully it helped shed more good light on the hearing-impaired community.

In June I was sitting in first class on a flight back to Seattle when I saw this guy in a Marine uniform. He was up front talking to a flight attendant. I mentioned earlier how at every game after the national anthem is sung, I salute in honor of our military. That's genuinely how I feel about our troops. So I went up to him and introduced myself and we talked a bit. His name was Stoney, and he'd originally been in the Navy but had switched over to the Marines. He asked about football, and I told him that what he was doing was hard work, and what I was doing was fun by comparison.

As a team, we have honor coins that we can give out to people in the military, but I didn't have any of them on me. Then an idea popped into my mind. I asked Stoney if he'd allow me to give him a small token of appreciation for what he was doing for our country—take my first-class seat in exchange for his seat back in coach. He refused at first, saying he couldn't do that, but when I persisted, he agreed.

I just wanted to brighten his day, nothing special. The flight attendant told me later that Stoney was smiling the whole time he was up in first class. The media somehow got ahold of that story, and it made the rounds afterward, but that wasn't why I did it. To me, it was no big deal. I wasn't seeking publicity. It was only a couple of hours in a plane. Members of the military aren't making much money, and bullets are coming at them. It's an incredibly hard job, and their sacrifices allow us to lead the lives we want to live in freedom. So it was a pleasure for me to switch seats with him.

Looking back on it now, that seemed a good way to cap off an epic Super Bowl season. Play hard and live with respect. It's tough to go wrong when you're doing both those things.

16

MY FOOT, THE FUTURE,
AND YOU

The OTAs came around to prepare for the start of the 2014 season. For two months it was a lot of running, lifting, meeting coaches, and learning plays. Then you put on helmets and do some practices. Mike Robinson retired, so the Hawks were going to go with me as their starting fullback, although they brought in another guy to compete with me at the start. That's the way football is. Even if you've got a starting position, you always need to fight to keep it. In football, the only thing you're guaranteed is *not* to be guaranteed a spot.

I had some good OTAs and learned more about the position of fullback. I could see things quicker and take it to the next level. That helps the offense if you understand what the guy next to you is doing, too.

On June 19, we had a ceremony where we finally got our Super Bowl rings. It was a big gathering. Usher performed, but I left early and unfortunately missed that.

Training camp came around and we put on our pads and started to hit hard. It was the real deal then. You're one of ninety guys again, all trying to make the team. Only fifty-three will make it in the end. I had a good camp and felt more confident overall. I didn't think of myself as great, but I got out there and made good tackles and got the job done. I stayed in close contact with Mike Robinson, who went to work as a network analyst. He'd played the position of fullback for a long time, and he gave me a lot of good tips about playing the position well, staying around, and lasting in the league.

The preseason began and right away we lost to the Broncos 21–16. I think they were getting back at us for the Super Bowl, but you never know. Each year is a new year. We beat the San Diego Chargers the next week 41–14, then beat the Chicago Bears 34–6. We ended the preseason by losing to the Oakland Raiders 41–31.

Our first regular season game was against the Green Bay Packers. It was one of the best games I'd ever had in terms of blocking. I rolled my ankle earlier in the week, so I had them tape it up and I kept playing. My ankle was hurting, but you've got to tough it out.

Near the end of the game, we had the ball on fourth and one. Coach called a play and I ran the route. Russell threw me the ball. I caught it, took off, and walked into the end zone. It was my second touchdown in the NFL. I kept the ball and gave it to my father, who was in the stands that day. That felt really good to score another league touchdown. The way I look at it, in high school I scored a lot of touchdowns, in college a few less, in the NFL so far—two. I wanted to remember the moment, but didn't want it to be my last touchdown, either.

After the game, the doc took a quick X-ray of my ankle, which was fine. But he told me I had what's called a "stress reaction" in my foot—in the fifth metatarsal (one of five long bones in the foot), to be exact. It's like a stress fracture that hasn't broken yet. I didn't even know it had happened. Actually, the reaction had happened the year before and was already healing. The doc said everything was fine but to keep an eye on it in case it got any worse.

So the season progressed, and I never had any problems with my foot. We lost to the Chargers in week two, then beat the Broncos in overtime. Week four was our bye, then we beat the Washington Redskins, then in week six lost to the Dallas Cowboys. Each game I was still taping my ankle, but that didn't bother me. The longer you progress in the NFL, you're bound to play with some sort of injury. Lots of guys are playing hurt every game. Your body wasn't made for fighting like that. I know a guy who doesn't have any cushion left in his knees, but he kept playing anyway. That's how this game rolls.

On October 19 we were set to play the St. Louis Rams. It was an away game, and at practice during the Wednesday before the game, I rolled my right ankle. I taped it and iced it and kept going anyway. My left foot started hurting, the one with the stress reaction. I guess it was taking more of the weight now to compensate for me being lighter on my right.

We headed to St. Louis. My ankle was still hurting, but it

wasn't bad. I was determined to play. During the warm-up before the game I ran a flat route and the practice quarterback threw the ball slightly in front of me. I reached out to get it, pushed off my left foot, and felt a *click-click*. I was like, *What the heck?!* My foot was throbbing.

At first I thought it was just a pulled muscle and I needed to walk it off. So I ran a few more routes. My foot was absolutely killing me by then. On one route I ran the other direction and needed to drive hard to the left, off my right foot. I pushed off with my left and tried to push up, but my foot went really weak. I still wasn't ready to accept that something was wrong with my foot. I told the trainer to tape my foot good. He said "no problem" and we went over to the table, where I took my shoe off and he started taping up my foot.

Right before I put my sock back on, the trainer moved my pinky toe and a shooting pain went up my leg. He saw me wince and put his hands in the middle of my foot on the outsides and moved it slightly. On a scale of 0 to 10, the pain was a 15. I was ready to kick him. He's like, "Yeah, something's not right."

He called for a cart. They came and got me, and we went to the X-ray room at the stadium. When the X-ray was examined, the doc let out a low whistle. It turned out that my stress reaction was now a full-blown stress fracture.

Hoo, man, we weren't even playing in the game yet. Of all the crazy things. I was out of that day's game for sure. I might be out for the whole season. I tried to call my mom, but she wasn't in, so I called my dad. He was at my grandma's house, getting ready to watch the game. I told him, then called my mom back.

"I broke my foot," was all I said.

Then I started crying.

Yeah, it was painful. I couldn't touch the ground with my foot. But it was more than that. We'd trained so much. I'd worked so hard to get to this point. And now I couldn't go out there and help the guys I worked hard with. Everybody's got their role, but I couldn't do mine. We lost that game against the Rams, 28–26. I felt like I'd let down my team.

There was nothing anybody could do. My only thought now was how I could get my foot healthy. I needed surgery, so I flew back to Seattle. We found the best foot doctor in the country and scheduled an appointment for two days later. He was in North Carolina, so I flew out there and had the operation. They drilled a hole into my foot and put a screw in there. The bone will heal around the screw, and it will be inside me for the rest of my life. Recovery was estimated at four to six weeks. A couple of days later, I flew home.

The Seahawks had a decision to make. They ended up putting me on the injured reserve, meaning I was temporarily unable to play. If a player is put on IR, it frees up a new spot on the team, so the team can add a new player. It also means that you can't practice or play for the rest of the regular season. So that was it for me. My 2014 season was officially over after six regular season games (and I'd only suited up for the sixth—not played in it). Tailback Robert Turbin stepped in for a game or two to play fullback, but when I was officially put on IR, the Seahawks brought over Will Tukuafu from the 49ers to take over for me. I'd still be around to help out wherever I could. I didn't want to sit at home and be mad or stew about it, but I was officially not playing.

Strange timing. My birthday is October 18. In the 2013 season when I injured my hamstring, the injury happened one day earlier, on October 17. In 2014 my broken foot happened one day later, on October 19. At age twenty-four, maybe it was my body's way of telling me that I was already getting a little old to play in the NFL.

So that's where I am as I'm writing the last pages of this book. I'm sitting on IR, wondering what's going to happen next. Sure, I'm thinking about life after football. Nobody can play in the NFL forever. But I don't think I'm done yet. I want to come back hard and play again.

When I look at things in perspective, my broken foot is only a minor setback. Looking back, I've been through a lot in life already. Kids teasing me when I was young. People not understanding me. People calling me names. People hurting me. But I always overcame. Sure, this is the first time my season has been ended by an injury, but I look at it as just another obstacle, one more thing to overcome. I can't give any excuses. I've just got to go do it. Life's like that. It's going to present you with obstacles every day, day in, day out. How you respond to those obstacles is going to determine a lot of your success.

Every time I go on the field, I prepare myself both mentally and spiritually. That hasn't changed since high school. Every time I come out of the tunnel, I'll go to the end zone, kneel, and pray. If my mom is in the stands, then she's on her feet, holding up her hand in prayer along with me. Our hearts are at a standstill then, at rest before God. He's the one who's setting the course of my life ultimately. After I pray, I get up and do what I need to do.

You know what I consider success?

Sure, the Super Bowl. But that's only one marker. It's more like this. A few years back, me and a bunch of my friends went up to the cabin at Lake Arrowhead that's owned by Brian's parents. It was me and Brian and Derek and Josh, I think. We were all on Brian's boat, and a few of us went wakeboarding. Then we were just hanging out, relaxing by the lake, enjoying the day. Brian and Derek got the bright idea that it would be funny to push everybody else in the water. So I was one of the first in. They completely surprised me, and when I came up splashing I was like, "What are you guys doing?!" because I still had my hearing aids in.

I could see the astonished looks on their faces. They know I can't go into the water like that. So we tried to dry out my hearing aids. Eventually they worked again. Pretty soon we were all laughing about it. But you know what was so great about that moment?

They'd forgotten I was deaf.

It wasn't an issue for them. That's what stood out in my mind. In their eyes, I wasn't a person with a disability. I was just their friend Derrick—a good friend. Somebody they cared about enough to horse around with like that.

In the big picture of things, that's success. It's when you're able to be just who you are and you're hanging out with the people who care about you. You've worked through your issues, and so have they. They accept you, and you accept them. You're friends for the long haul, and nothing's going to change that.

My friend Brandon had a good friend who passed away, and

naturally he took it really hard. This was back in May 2013, and I knew the whole experience was messing with him. I didn't know what to do, so one day I just drove by his house and picked him up. I didn't want him to stay home all day. I brought him back to my house to be with other friends.

"I'm here for you, if you ever need anything," I said. "I've always got your back. I know it sucks right now, but things are going to get better. Just remember all the people who love you and care for you. If you ever want to talk, I'm here for you."

That's success. To stop what you're doing and be there for a friend. I know Brandon would do the same for me. I wanted to do that for him.

Here's success: There's an outfit in Los Angeles, called Ear-ables, that helps children get prosthetic ears, and I've done some work with them before. It's an amazing company. Some of the kids they work with are born without ears, but the company can create ears now that actually grow along with a child. We did an event there this past summer, and all these kids were talking to me afterward.

I didn't think much about this at the time, but my agent Derrick Fox was there, and at one point he said, "Hey, do you know where your Super Bowl ring is right now?"

I shrugged and motioned my head in the direction of a crowd of kids. One boy had asked if he could take a look at it, and he'd grown so enamored with it that he'd wandered off. He was in another group of kids, and they were all trying it on their fingers. We were all having so much fun, I didn't really think too much about it. Derrick works with a lot of other professional athletes and celebrities and he knows they can sometimes be aloof or whatever, so he was like, "That's pretty cool—what you're doing for those kids. This is a moment they'll never forget. Trying on your ring like that."

That's success. Caring about people more than things. Being kind to everybody you meet. Letting them try on your ring if they want.

My audiologist Nancy Adzovich has worked with me since I was in middle school. She sits on the board of my foundation today. For years she worked to help me overcome. A few years back, she was working with an eighth-grade student who was being bullied because he was hard of hearing. Nancy texted my mom and asked if next time I got a break in my schedule I could come meet with the boy to encourage him a bit. We all met at the Cheesecake Factory in the Brea Mall for lunch—Nancy, my mom and me, the boy and his mom. No cameras. It was just us talking about how to make it in life.

We talked and talked, and for the first time in a long while, I guess, that boy was smiling, taking it all in. When we finished up, Nancy looked at me and said, "Do you realize that we've been talking for three hours?"

In fact, I didn't realize that. I just wanted to help this kid.

That's success.

Here's what I want to say. Everybody has problems in life. Maybe it's hearing problems. Or vision problems. Or depression. Or ADHD. Everybody needs to overcome something. You gotta aim high to make it over those problems. You gotta give it your all.

The responsibility is yours. It might seem like you've been chipping away at that problem for a lot of years and you're no closer to a solution. But it's like that picture of a guy digging for diamonds. He's been digging for years and has found nothing and wants to give up. But if you could just pull back to see what's under the earth, the diamonds are really close. He's only an inch away from his destination.

Think back to what you wanted to be when you were a kid. What really excited you then? Maybe it was politics. More than anything, you wanted to be president. Then that's the direction you should go today. Maybe you will never become president. But if you set your sights high, maybe you'll be a congressman or a mayor. Or maybe you'll volunteer to help the next president succeed. Life is too short to settle for excuses. If you settle for excuses, then you'll always arrive at second best. Aim for your dreams, don't doubt yourself, don't let anyone tell you that you're a failure, and put in the work.

When I sign autographs these days, I always sign my name and two other things—"No excuses" and "Be yourself." What I mean by that is don't worry about the naysayers. People will always tell you that you can't do something. Don't listen to them. Or do use what the naysayers say as fuel to push you forward. If somebody tells you that you can't do something, let that motivate you to prove people wrong. I decided years ago that if someone told me I couldn't do something, I'd just say, "Watch me."

Life is going to be hard. You're going to have obstacles. You might win the Super Bowl only to break your foot a short time later. That's how life goes. Up and down. Down and up. You always have to keep going up.

On my back I have a tattoo that says "God's son," along with a picture of a cross. On the bottom of the tattoo it says, "May the strongest survive." God gives assignments to His toughest soldiers. God wants you to overcome. You gotta have faith to depend on God for your ultimate success. So work hard and don't give any excuses.

That's the final thing I'd want anybody to remember—that powerful mindset—that you've got what it takes.

As I've been saying all along, there are no excuses. Your best is yet to come.

AFTERWORD

Right before this book was to go to press, the publisher asked me to share a few last-minute thoughts about the Hawks' heartbreaker of a loss to the Patriots in Super Bowl XLIX.

I was still on IR, standing on the sidelines for the Super Bowl along with the players watching the game, just trying to do whatever I could to encourage them on. My foot has healed well, but being on IR meant I was out the whole season—including not being able to play in the Super Bowl. That was tough to take, but it had to be done.

After the surgery on my foot, I did as much rehab as I could take, flying back and forth between L.A. and Seattle, doing rehab in both places. IR guys aren't allowed to travel with the team to away games, so I'd go to every home game and be in the team suite with the other IR players and sometimes down on the field, cheering the guys on and just helping them any way I could. When I'm out on the field, I always appreciate it if I can get little bits of info from the guys on the sidelines. It's a different kind of focus, and the players on the sidelines can see things a player on the field often can't. By mid-December 2014, doctors told me I was at 90 percent. Then in early January 2015, two weeks before we played the Packers on the eighteenth for the NFC title, I was officially declared "healed" and cleared to play.

Because I was on IR, I still couldn't play in any games for the rest of the season, of course. But that NFC championship game was amazing, if you remember. It was the one where we came from behind in the fourth quarter.

We'd beaten the Packers at the start of the season (the game where I had my touchdown) and there was no doubt in my mind that we could beat them again. But I think we got too confident in the NFC championship game. We couldn't find our rhythm at first and were down 16–0 at the half. That stunk.

The second half began, and the offense still wasn't producing much, and when that happens, there's only so much the defense can do. It goes that way for any team. For three and a half quarters not much was going on. Finally, four minutes were left in the game, and we were down 19–7.

But there's something we always say about Russell Wilson: There's nothing that man can't handle. He keeps believing. For him, nothing's impossible. Even that late in the game, Russell started connecting with receivers, and something just flipped for us. Maybe it was that strong will within ourselves that can get renewed at a moment's notice. Nobody knows quite what caused the spark, but as a team, we became furious. I think we all decided that if we were going to lose, we were going to go down fighting.

With just over three minutes to go in the fourth quarter, Russell connected with Doug Baldwin and then with Marshawn Lynch for a touchdown, which was called back because Marshawn stepped out. It didn't matter. Marshawn ran up the middle four yards. Russell scrambled to the one-yard line, then on the next play took it into the end zone. And suddenly the score was 19–14.

Two minutes were left, and we were set to kick off to the Packers. That doesn't sound like much time, but two minutes can actually be a long time in a football game. We kicked off, a wobbling onside kick that our receiver Chris Matthews fortunately recovered. Marshawn had a long run on one of the next plays and took it all the way in for another touchdown. Russell scrambled around and threw to our tight end, Luke Willson, for a two-point conversion, and suddenly we were winning this game, 22–19.

But like I say, anything can happen in the last minutes of a game. The Packers had the ball again, and with nineteen seconds they had it close enough to kick a field goal. The score was tied at 22. We headed into overtime. Russell drove the offense hard down the field and connected with Kearse to win the game, 28–22. The crowd went nuts. The Seahawks were headed to the Super Bowl again—second year in a row!

The Super Bowl was set for February 1, 2015, in Glendale, Arizona. The Hawks left a week early to get there before Sunday's game. The IR guys don't get there until Thursday, so I actually drove home to Orange County early, me and my dog and my clothes.

I knew the season would be over after the game, so I wanted to get my truck and my dog home.

On Thursday I drove to Phoenix. My agents had some interviews lined up for me, so I needed to get out there early in the morning. Everybody was asking about last year and if we could repeat. My answer more than once was "We're going to find out. Nobody really knows until we get there."

Right before the game, I was talking to a teammate and we were both saying that something felt different this year compared to last, but we couldn't figure it out. We talked for about five minutes and then it dawned on us—last year we'd never won a Super Bowl, but this year we had. Last year we'd been so hungry. We were still hungry this year, but it was a different kind of hunger. It was a different kind of excitement. We had the confidence to know we belonged. We were strong. We weren't going to settle for anything less than a win.

When the game began, we were confident. The Patriots were the number-one seed in their conference, and we were the number one in ours. Our coach, Pete Carroll, used to coach the Patriots, from 1997 to 1999, and had won an AFC division title with them in 1997, but it was a different team now. At halftime we were in a dead tie: 14–14. Katy Perry and Lenny Kravitz performed the halftime show, then we were on again.

By the fourth quarter we were up 24–14 and playing confidently. But the Patriots quarterback, Tom Brady, pressed hard and connected with his receivers on two big drives to bring the score to 28–24 for them, with just over two minutes left to play. Everything was still okay. Nobody on the Hawks had been celebrating when we were up, and nobody was panicking now that we were down. We knew the game was going to be won in the final five minutes. We needed to keep our heads and keep fighting.

The ball was ours. This was our big chance. First and second downs ended with Russell throwing incompletions. But third down, same ten yards to go, he connected with Ricardo Lockette for eleven yards. Russell threw hard to Kearse on the next play, and the ball was deflected by a Patriots player, but Kearse caught it anyway—while lying on his back!

So just like that, there was just over a minute left to play and we were on the Patriots five-yard line with a first down. On the next play, Lynch rammed the ball to the one-yard line and we ran the clock down to twenty-six seconds. We were poised to score and win the game.

But what happened on the final play for us caught everybody unaware. It was one of those things you had to blink twice at because you thought you were seeing things. We threw an interception. *Bam!* And just like that, New England had the ball. There were still a few seconds on the clock, but the game was all but over. We lost, 28–24.

Everybody was stunned. And of course everybody had an opinion afterward about that heartbreaking play. Every fan and commentator was insisting that we should have run the ball. Sure, it's easy for people to say that in hindsight. But at the same time, nobody would have been telling the Hawks to keep the ball on the ground if we'd won. Why did the interception happen? We can speculate forever, but I'd say it's just football, and interceptions are one of those things. Sometimes you win, sometimes you lose.

Afterward we were devastated as a team. And angry. All that work we did and we couldn't pull through. But here's what I want to say with these final words of the book.

That loss is already behind us. Already we're thinking about next year, and we know we're going to be strong. We're working out, focusing our minds, and we know we're coming back hungry. We know what it feels like to lose a Super Bowl. And we know what it feels like to win a Super Bowl. We want to win again, and we'll do everything in our power to achieve that goal. That's the vow.

Because there are no excuses.

Hey—I'll see you next year.

—Derrick Coleman Jr.

ACKNOWLEDGMENTS

I have so many people to thank who've encouraged me, challenged me, supported me, and helped me over the years.

I want to send enormous thanks to my parents, Derrick Coleman Sr. and May Hamlin, for always believing in me. Huge thanks also go to my brother, Keyon, and sister, Tenisha, my grandparents, my aunts and uncles, my cousins, and all my extended family.

To all my friends. You mean the world to me.

To all my coaches over the years. Thank you so much for encouraging me to become the best.

Thanks to all my fellow players. We're in this together.

Thanks to my audiologist, Nancy Adzovich, and all the board members of the Derrick L. Coleman Jr. No Excuse Foundation.

Thanks to my sports agents, Mark Bloom and Derrick Fox; my

ACKNOWLEDGMENTS

literary agent, Steve Fisher; my editor, Adam Wilson, and all the team at Jeter Publishing. Thanks to collaborative writer Marcus Brotherton and his research assistant, Matt Weeda.

Thanks to all the fans. Without you, this would all be impossible.

Finally, all thanks go to God, the King of all glory, Lord of all.

ABOUT THE AUTHOR

Derrick Coleman Jr. is a fullback for the Super Bowl XLVIII champion Seattle Seahawks. He made history by becoming the first deaf offensive player in the NFL, and he is the first ever deaf player to win a Super Bowl.

Derrick played college football for UCLA, where he rushed for more than 1,100 yards in his final two seasons with the Bruins, scoring eleven touchdowns in his senior year alone. Undrafted, Derrick signed as a free agent with the Minnesota Vikings, then with the Seahawks a year later.

Off the field, Derrick uses his charisma and celebrity status to encourage people to pursue their dreams despite obstacles that inevitably arise. He is the founder and CEO of the Derrick L. Coleman Jr. No Excuse Foundation, an organization that advocates for the hearing-impaired community as well as working to lessen instances of bullying.

Derrick was featured in an enormously popular Duracell battery commercial as well as a viral YouTube video where two nine-year-olds with hearing impairments met him and received Super Bowl tickets.

For more information, see his website: www.derricklcoleman.com

---

ABOUT THE COLLABORATIVE AUTHOR

Marcus Brotherton is a journalist and professional writer known internationally for his books and literary collaborations with high-profile public figures, humanitarians, inspirational leaders, and military personnel.

He has authored or coauthored more than twenty-five books, including the critically acclaimed *Feast for Thieves*, the much-loved *Finding Martha's Place*, and the *New York Times* bestseller *We Who Are Alive and Remain* with twenty of the original Band of Brothers.

For more information, see his website: www.marcusbrotherton.com